Combating Anxiety for Teens 101: A Parent's Guide -

Overcoming Social and Personal Anxiety and Stress

By Avi Quinn

Table of Contents:

This comprehensive 40-page, 10,000-word book provides a thorough exploration of anxiety relief for teenagers, offering practical strategies and guidance to help them overcome anxiety and stress. Through a combination of science-based information, real-life examples, and actionable exercises, this book aims to empower teens with the tools they need to navigate the challenges of adolescence while fostering resilience and emotional well-being.

Introduction

Introduction

Section 1: Understanding Teen Anxiety

In the labyrinthine world of adolescence, where dreams intertwine with insecurities and youthful exuberance dances with the weight of responsibility, anxiety can often take center stage. It is a silent, pervasive presence, lurking in the minds of countless teenagers, casting shadows on their path to self-discovery. Understanding teen anxiety is the first step towards illuminating those shadows and guiding our adolescents towards the radiant future they deserve.

Teenagers today face a myriad of challenges that previous generations might never have imagined. The relentless onslaught of social media, academic pressures, peer dynamics, and the perpetual quest for self-identity can all serve as breeding grounds for anxiety. As parents, educators, mentors, and caregivers, it's crucial for us to delve deep into the realm of teen anxiety, decipher its intricacies, and learn how to be empathetic allies in our teens' journey towards emotional well-being.

Section 2: The Importance of Addressing Teen Anxiety

In our bustling, technology-driven society, the pace of life seems to have quickened, leaving many adolescents feeling as though they are sprinting a marathon. Amidst this frenetic pace, it's easy to overlook or trivialize the anxieties that teenagers grapple with daily. However, understanding that these anxieties are not mere passing phases but potent forces capable of shaping a teenager's life is paramount.

Addressing teen anxiety is not a luxury; it's an imperative. The emotional well-being of our teenagers impacts not only their immediate happiness but also their long-term success and overall health. Unaddressed anxiety can lead to a cascade of negative consequences, from diminished academic performance to strained relationships and even physical health issues. Yet, with the right tools, knowledge, and support, we can equip our teens to not only survive but thrive in this complex world.

This book embarks on a journey to explore the multifaceted landscape of teen anxiety, offering insights, strategies, and practical guidance to help teens, parents, educators, and anyone invested in the well-being of our younger generation. Together, we will uncover the secrets of adolescent anxiety and discover the means to foster resilience, emotional growth, and brighter tomorrows for our teens.

Chapter 1: The Anatomy of Teen Anxiety

Section 1: What is Anxiety?

At its core, anxiety is a natural and adaptive response designed to keep us safe in the face of perceived threats. It's that rush of adrenaline that heightens our senses when we sense danger, like encountering a wild animal in the woods. Anxiety can be a friend, warning us of potential risks and helping us prepare for challenges. However, in the complex world of adolescence, anxiety often morphs into a formidable foe.

Teen anxiety is not the fleeting worry or unease that all of us experience from time to time; it's a persistent, intense, and sometimes overwhelming state of apprehension. It's the knot in the stomach before a big exam, the social unease at a school dance, or the paralyzing fear of public speaking. In essence, anxiety becomes problematic when it disrupts daily life, interferes with relationships, and prevents teenagers from pursuing their goals and dreams.

Understanding the nuances of anxiety is crucial for both teenagers and those who support them. We'll explore the various facets of anxiety, from its physical manifestations to its emotional toll, and we'll uncover how it can become a formidable adversary that demands our attention and action.

Section 2: Types of Anxiety Disorders

Anxiety is not a one-size-fits-all experience; it wears many masks and manifests in diverse forms. Anxiety disorders are clinical conditions characterized by excessive and persistent worry, fear, or anxiety. In the realm of teen anxiety, several common disorders stand out, each with its unique set of challenges.

- **Generalized Anxiety Disorder (GAD)**: Teens with GAD often experience excessive worry about various aspects of their lives, including academic performance, relationships, and their future. This constant state of apprehension can be mentally and physically draining.

- **Social Anxiety Disorder (SAD)**: SAD can turn social interactions into minefields for teenagers. The fear of judgment, embarrassment, or rejection can be so overwhelming that it leads to avoidance of social situations, which can hinder personal growth and development.
- **Panic Disorder**: Teens with panic disorder may suffer from sudden and intense panic attacks, characterized by symptoms like a racing heart, shortness of breath, and a feeling of impending doom. The unpredictability of these attacks can be particularly distressing.
- **Specific Phobias**: From the fear of heights (acrophobia) to the fear of spiders (arachnophobia), specific phobias can manifest in countless ways. For teens, these phobias can interfere with everyday life and limit their experiences.
- **Obsessive-Compulsive Disorder (OCD)**: OCD involves recurring, intrusive thoughts (obsessions) and repetitive behaviors (compulsions). Teens with OCD may find themselves trapped in rituals that temporarily alleviate anxiety but ultimately maintain its grip.

Recognizing these different anxiety disorders and their unique characteristics is vital for early intervention and appropriate support. By shedding light on the specific challenges each disorder presents, we can better equip teenagers to manage their anxiety effectively.

Section 3: Common Triggers for Teen Anxiety

Teenagers live at the crossroads of childhood and adulthood, navigating a multitude of changes and challenges. Amidst this transformative journey, numerous triggers can exacerbate anxiety and push it to the forefront of their lives. Identifying these common triggers is a critical step in understanding and addressing teen anxiety.

- **Academic Pressures**: The relentless pursuit of high grades, college admissions, and the fear of failure can create immense academic stress. Teens often internalize these pressures, leading to anxiety about their performance and future prospects.
- **Peer and Social Pressures**: Adolescence is a time of identity formation and fitting in. The fear of rejection, social comparison, and the desire to conform to societal norms can weigh heavily on teenagers, triggering anxiety.

- **Family Dynamics**: Family conflicts, parental expectations, and changes in family structures can contribute to anxiety in teens. High-conflict households or a lack of support can be especially challenging.
- **Social Media and Technology**: The digital age has introduced a new realm of social interaction and comparison through social media. The curated lives displayed online can lead to unrealistic expectations and feelings of inadequacy.
- **Life Transitions**: Adolescents undergo a series of significant life transitions, such as moving to a new school, starting college, or experiencing the physical changes of puberty. These transitions can evoke anxiety about the unknown.
- **Traumatic Events**: Witnessing or experiencing traumatic events, such as accidents, violence, or natural disasters, can trigger anxiety in teenagers. The emotional aftermath of such events can linger long after the initial shock.

Understanding these common triggers for teen anxiety provides a foundation for intervention and support. By recognizing the sources of anxiety, teenagers and their caregivers can work together to develop strategies for coping and resilience, ultimately empowering teens to navigate the tumultuous path of adolescence with greater ease.

Chapter 2: Recognizing Anxiety in Teens

Teenagers are complex beings, and their experiences can often be shrouded in mystery. Understanding anxiety in teens requires a keen eye and an empathetic heart. In this chapter, we will delve into the signs and symptoms of teen anxiety, explore the impact of social media and technology, and uncover the intricate connection between physical and mental health.

Section 1: Signs and Symptoms

Teenagers may not always express their emotions and struggles verbally, making it imperative to recognize the subtle and not-so-subtle signs of anxiety. Here are some common signs and symptoms to look out for:

- **Physical Symptoms**: Teens with anxiety may experience headaches, stomachaches, muscle tension, and fatigue. These physical manifestations are often the body's way of responding to stress.
- **Emotional Changes**: Anxiety can lead to a rollercoaster of emotions. Teens may become irritable, easily agitated, or excessively worried about everyday issues. Mood swings and tearfulness can also be indicative of underlying anxiety.
- **Behavioral Changes**: Watch for changes in behavior. Avoidance of social situations, schoolwork, or responsibilities can signal anxiety. Some teens may withdraw from activities they once enjoyed.
- **Sleep Disturbances**: Anxiety often disrupts sleep patterns. Teens may have trouble falling asleep, staying asleep, or experience frequent nightmares. Sleep deprivation can exacerbate anxiety symptoms.
- **Academic Challenges**: A decline in academic performance, even in capable students, can be a red flag. Anxiety may impair concentration, memory, and the ability to complete tasks.
- **Social Isolation**: Teens with anxiety may withdraw from friends and social activities, choosing isolation over potential social stressors. They may fear judgment or criticism from peers.
- **Perfectionism**: Striving for perfection can be a mask for anxiety. Teens may set unrealistically high standards for themselves, fearing the consequences of falling short.

- **Physical Restlessness**: Some teens may exhibit restlessness or fidgeting as a way to cope with their anxious energy. This can manifest as nail-biting, hair twirling, or leg shaking.

Recognizing these signs and symptoms is the first step in helping teens address their anxiety. It's essential to approach them with empathy and open communication, creating a safe space for them to express their feelings and concerns.

Section 2: The Role of Social Media and Technology

The digital age has ushered in unprecedented connectivity and opportunities for self-expression, but it has also brought new challenges, especially for teens grappling with anxiety.

- **Constant Comparison**: Social media platforms often serve as highlight reels of others' lives, fostering unrealistic comparisons. Teens may feel inadequate or anxious when measuring themselves against curated online personas.
- **Cyberbullying**: The digital realm can be a breeding ground for cyberbullying, where hurtful comments and harassment can intensify anxiety. The anonymity of the internet can embolden bullies.
- **Fear of Missing Out (FOMO)**: The fear of missing out on social events or experiences documented online can trigger anxiety. Teens may feel pressure to constantly engage with social media to avoid missing out.
- **Digital Detox**: Paradoxically, the very technology that contributes to anxiety can also offer solutions. Encouraging periodic digital detoxes can help teens break free from the cycle of comparison and information overload.

Understanding the complexities of social media and technology in the context of teen anxiety is crucial for both teens and their caregivers. Balancing the benefits of connectivity with mindful tech use can mitigate some of the negative effects.

Section 3: The Connection Between Physical and Mental Health

The mind and body are intricately connected, and this connection is particularly significant in the realm of anxiety.

- **Physical Effects of Anxiety**: Anxiety can manifest in physical symptoms such as increased heart rate, shallow breathing, muscle tension, and digestive issues. Understanding these physical manifestations as signs of anxiety can help teens better manage their condition.
- **The Role of Exercise**: Regular physical activity has been shown to reduce anxiety by releasing endorphins, the body's natural mood elevators. Encouraging teens to engage in physical activity can be an effective strategy for anxiety management.
- **Diet and Nutrition**: Nutritional choices can impact mood and anxiety levels. A diet rich in fruits, vegetables, whole grains, and lean proteins can support both physical and mental well-being.
- **Sleep and Anxiety**: Poor sleep quality or insufficient sleep can exacerbate anxiety symptoms. Establishing healthy sleep routines is essential for managing anxiety in teens.
- **The Mind-Body Connection**: Practices such as mindfulness, yoga, and deep breathing exercises can help teens connect with their bodies and reduce anxiety. These techniques promote relaxation and emotional regulation.

Understanding how physical and mental health intersect can provide a holistic approach to addressing teen anxiety. By paying attention to the body's cues and nurturing both physical and emotional well-being, teens can embark on a journey towards greater balance and resilience.

Chapter 3: The Impact of Anxiety on Teenagers

Anxiety is not an isolated emotion; it ripples through various facets of a teenager's life, affecting academic performance, relationships, physical health, and self-esteem. In this chapter, we will explore how anxiety can cast its shadow on these crucial aspects of a teenager's well-being.

Section 1: Academic Performance

The classroom can be a breeding ground for anxiety, and the pressure to excel academically can weigh heavily on teenagers.

- **Test Anxiety**: Anxiety often peaks during exams, leading to symptoms such as racing thoughts, sweaty palms, and difficulty concentrating. These physical and emotional reactions can hinder test performance.
- **Procrastination**: Fear of failure can lead to procrastination, as students may avoid tasks to escape the anxiety associated with them. This can result in poor time management and last-minute cramming.
- **Perfectionism**: Teens with anxiety may set impossibly high standards for themselves. While a desire for excellence is admirable, perfectionism can lead to unrealistic expectations and a fear of making mistakes.
- **Avoidance of Challenges**: Anxiety can discourage teens from taking on challenging academic tasks or pursuing their passions. The fear of not measuring up can stifle their intellectual growth.

By recognizing the impact of anxiety on academic performance, parents, educators, and teens themselves can work together to implement strategies that alleviate stress and foster a healthier approach to learning.

Section 2: Relationships

Navigating the turbulent waters of relationships is a fundamental part of adolescence, and anxiety can profoundly affect how teens form and maintain connections with others.

- **Social Isolation**: Anxiety can lead to social withdrawal, making it difficult for teenagers to engage with peers. This isolation can perpetuate feelings of loneliness and exacerbate anxiety.
- **Conflict Avoidance**: Teens with anxiety may avoid confrontations or expressing their needs in relationships, fearing rejection or criticism. This can lead to unfulfilling relationships and unresolved issues.
- **Overdependence**: Some teens may become overly reliant on a few close friends or family members, seeking constant reassurance and validation to quell their anxiety.
- **Jealousy and Insecurity**: Anxiety can fuel jealousy and insecurity in relationships, causing teens to constantly doubt their worth and the intentions of those around them.

Recognizing how anxiety influences relationships is crucial for fostering healthy connections. Encouraging open communication, empathy, and teaching conflict resolution skills can help teenagers build strong and supportive relationships.

Section 3: Physical Health

Anxiety takes a toll on not just the mind but also the body. Understanding the physical implications of anxiety is essential for the overall well-being of teenagers.

- **Sleep Disturbances**: Anxiety can disrupt sleep patterns, leading to insomnia or frequent awakenings during the night. The resulting sleep deprivation can exacerbate anxiety symptoms.
- **Nutritional Impact**: Some teens may turn to comfort eating or restrict their diet due to anxiety. These behaviors can affect nutritional intake and physical health.
- **Headaches and Muscle Tension**: The physical symptoms of anxiety, such as headaches and muscle tension, can become chronic and lead to discomfort and decreased quality of life.
- **Stomach and Digestive Issues**: Anxiety can contribute to stomachaches, nausea, and digestive problems. The gut-brain connection plays a significant role in anxiety-related physical symptoms.

By recognizing the physical consequences of anxiety, teens can take proactive steps to prioritize their physical health, including proper nutrition, regular exercise, and practicing relaxation techniques.

Section 4: Self-Esteem

The lens through which teenagers view themselves can become distorted by anxiety, leading to low self-esteem and a negative self-image.

- **Negative Self-Talk**: Anxiety often fuels a constant stream of negative self-talk, where teens berate themselves for perceived shortcomings and mistakes.
- **Comparisons with Others**: The tendency to compare oneself unfavorably to others is exacerbated by anxiety. Teens may feel they are never good enough or that they do not measure up to their peers.
- **Self-Doubt**: Anxiety can erode self-confidence, causing teens to doubt their abilities and worth. This self-doubt can hinder personal growth and achievement.
- **Fear of Rejection**: Anxiety can lead to an intense fear of rejection or criticism, making it challenging for teens to put themselves out there and pursue their goals.

Recognizing the link between anxiety and self-esteem is crucial for building resilience and a positive self-image. Teens can learn to challenge negative self-talk, practice self-compassion, and embrace imperfection as a natural part of the human experience.

Chapter 4: The Teen Brain and Anxiety

The teenage years are a period of profound transformation, not only in the physical and emotional sense but also within the intricate landscape of the adolescent brain. In this chapter, we will embark on a journey through the developmental changes in the adolescent brain, explore the neurobiology of anxiety, and unravel the significant role hormones play in shaping the adolescent experience.

Section 1: How the Adolescent Brain Develops

Adolescence is a time of remarkable brain development, characterized by both structural and functional changes. Understanding this developmental process is crucial for comprehending how anxiety can manifest in the teenage brain.

- **Neuroplasticity**: The adolescent brain is highly adaptable, with a remarkable capacity for learning and change. This neuroplasticity allows teens to acquire new skills and knowledge rapidly but also makes them susceptible to the impact of stress and anxiety.
- **Frontal Lobe Development**: The frontal lobes, responsible for decision-making, impulse control, and emotional regulation, undergo significant development during adolescence. However, this development is uneven, leading to potential impulsivity and emotional volatility.
- **Peer Influence**: The desire for social acceptance and peer approval is closely tied to brain development. The brain's reward system is particularly active during adolescence, contributing to the significance of social connections.

Understanding the dynamic changes occurring in the adolescent brain can provide insight into why teens are particularly vulnerable to anxiety and how interventions can be tailored to their unique developmental needs.

Section 2: The Neurobiology of Anxiety

Anxiety is not solely a psychological phenomenon; it is deeply rooted in the neurobiology of the brain. Examining the brain's role in anxiety helps us comprehend its profound impact on teenagers.

- **The Amygdala**: The amygdala, a small almond-shaped structure in the brain, plays a central role in processing emotions, particularly fear and anxiety. It can become overactive in individuals with anxiety disorders, leading to heightened emotional responses.
- **The Prefrontal Cortex**: The prefrontal cortex, responsible for executive functions like decision-making and impulse control, interacts with the amygdala to regulate emotional responses. Dysregulation in this circuitry can contribute to anxiety.
- **Neurotransmitters**: Chemical messengers called neurotransmitters, such as serotonin and dopamine, play a significant role in anxiety. Imbalances in these neurotransmitters can affect mood and contribute to anxiety symptoms.
- **Brain Circuits**: Anxiety is associated with specific brain circuits responsible for threat detection and stress response. These circuits can become hypersensitive in individuals with anxiety disorders.

Understanding the neurobiology of anxiety helps demystify this complex condition and highlights the importance of addressing both psychological and neurological aspects in treatment and support for anxious teenagers.

Section 3: How Hormones Play a Role

Hormonal changes are a hallmark of adolescence, and these fluctuations exert a profound influence on the teenage brain and the experience of anxiety.

- **Puberty and Hormonal Surge**: The onset of puberty triggers significant hormonal changes, including the release of sex hormones like estrogen and testosterone. These changes can influence mood and emotional regulation.
- **Stress Hormones**: The release of stress hormones, such as cortisol, is a natural response to stressors. However, chronic stress and anxiety can lead to dysregulation of these hormones, contributing to anxiety disorders.

- **Gender Differences**: Hormonal changes in adolescence differ between genders, contributing to variations in the prevalence and presentation of anxiety disorders. Understanding these differences is vital for tailored approaches to anxiety management.
- **Hormones and Brain Development**: Hormones play a role in shaping the adolescent brain. The interaction between hormones and brain development can influence emotional responses and vulnerability to anxiety.

Recognizing the impact of hormones on anxiety is essential for understanding the unique challenges faced by teenagers during this developmental stage. It also underscores the need for holistic approaches to anxiety management that address both hormonal and psychological factors.

Chapter 5: Coping Mechanisms and Their Pitfalls

In the intricate dance of managing anxiety, adolescents often resort to coping mechanisms as a means of finding relief and control. However, not all coping strategies are healthy or effective. This chapter explores common avoidance strategies, self-medication, and the long-term consequences of these approaches in dealing with teen anxiety.

Section 1: Avoidance Strategies

Avoidance is a natural instinct when facing something perceived as threatening or anxiety-inducing. In the short term, avoidance may provide temporary relief, but it often exacerbates anxiety in the long run.

- **Social Avoidance**: Teens with social anxiety may avoid social situations, leading to isolation and missed opportunities for personal growth and connection.
- **Academic Avoidance**: Anxiety about schoolwork can lead to procrastination and avoidance, which can result in poor academic performance and increased stress.
- **Avoidance of Triggers**: Teens may steer clear of situations or places that trigger their anxiety, limiting their experiences and potentially reinforcing their fears.

Recognizing avoidance as a coping mechanism is crucial because it can perpetuate anxiety and hinder a teenager's ability to confront and manage their fears effectively.

Section 2: Self-Medication

Some teenagers turn to self-medication as a way to numb or escape their anxious feelings. This can manifest in various forms, including substance abuse and risky behaviors.

- **Substance Abuse**: Alcohol, drugs, and even prescription medications are sometimes used to self-medicate anxiety symptoms. While they may provide temporary relief, they often lead to addiction and worsened mental health.
- **Unhealthy Coping Behaviors**: Teens may engage in risky behaviors such as self-harm, reckless driving, or unsafe sexual practices as a way to cope with anxiety. These behaviors can have severe physical and emotional consequences.
- **Emotional Eating**: Some teenagers may turn to food as a source of comfort, leading to unhealthy eating patterns and potential weight-related health issues.

Understanding the dangers of self-medication is crucial, as it can lead to a cycle of dependency and further exacerbate anxiety in the long term.

Section 3: The Long-Term Consequences

The short-term relief offered by avoidance strategies and self-medication often comes at a steep price. Over time, these coping mechanisms can lead to a range of long-term consequences that impact a teenager's mental and physical well-being.

- **Increased Anxiety**: Avoidance and self-medication do not address the root causes of anxiety. Instead, they reinforce avoidance behaviors and may lead to more severe anxiety disorders.
- **Substance Dependency**: Self-medication with drugs or alcohol can result in substance use disorders, which can be challenging to overcome and may require professional intervention.
- **Deteriorating Relationships**: Avoiding social interactions can strain relationships with friends and family, leading to feelings of isolation and loneliness.
- **Academic and Career Implications**: Chronic avoidance of academic challenges can limit future educational and career opportunities, hindering long-term success.
- **Physical Health Issues**: Self-medication and unhealthy coping behaviors can lead to physical health problems, including addiction, obesity, and other medical conditions.

Understanding the potential long-term consequences of these coping mechanisms underscores the importance of early intervention and support for anxious teenagers. By addressing anxiety in healthier ways and seeking professional help when needed, teens can pave the way for a brighter, more fulfilling future.

Chapter 6: The Power of Mindfulness

In a world filled with distractions and constant noise, mindfulness stands as a beacon of calm and clarity. This chapter explores mindfulness from its foundational principles to practical techniques and how to incorporate it into daily life.

Section 1: What is Mindfulness?

Mindfulness is more than just a buzzword; it's a profound way of living. In this section, we dive deep into the essence of mindfulness:

Defining Mindfulness: We break down the concept of mindfulness and explain what it means to be truly present in the moment.

Mindfulness is a practice of being fully present in the moment, without judgment or distraction. It involves paying attention to your thoughts, feelings, bodily sensations, and the environment around you with a sense of curiosity and acceptance.

Origins of Mindfulness Practices:

Explore the historical and cultural roots of mindfulness, including its origins in ancient meditation traditions

Mindfulness practices have a rich history rooted in ancient Eastern traditions, particularly Buddhism. Understanding their origins can provide valuable context for modern applications of mindfulness in anxiety relief.

- **Buddhist Roots**: Mindfulness, known as "sati" in Pali and "smṛti" in Sanskrit, is a fundamental concept in Buddhist philosophy and meditation. It has been practiced for over two millennia as a means to achieve insight, enlightenment, and liberation from suffering.

- **Thich Nhat Hanh**: In the 20th century, the Vietnamese Zen Buddhist monk Thich Nhat Hanh played a pivotal role in introducing mindfulness to the Western world. He coined the term "Engaged Buddhism" and popularized mindfulness as a secular practice accessible to people of all backgrounds.
- **Jon Kabat-Zinn**: Jon Kabat-Zinn, a pioneer in the field of mindfulness-based interventions, developed the Mindfulness-Based Stress Reduction (MBSR) program in the late 1970s. This program combined traditional mindfulness practices with modern psychological insights and made mindfulness more widely applicable, including to anxiety relief.
- **Mindfulness-Based Cognitive Therapy (MBCT)**: Building on MBSR, Mindfulness-Based Cognitive Therapy was developed to specifically target the recurrence of depression. It combines mindfulness practices with elements of cognitive therapy and has been adapted for various anxiety disorders.
- **Integration into Western Psychology**: Mindfulness practices have become an integral part of Western psychology and mental health treatments. They are recognized for their effectiveness in reducing anxiety, depression, and stress while promoting emotional well-being.
- **Secularization**: While rooted in Buddhist traditions, mindfulness practices have been secularized, making them accessible to individuals from diverse cultural and religious backgrounds. This inclusivity has contributed to their widespread adoption for anxiety relief.
- **Scientific Research**: The application of mindfulness in psychological and neurological research has grown significantly. Studies have demonstrated the positive effects of mindfulness on brain function, emotional regulation, and overall mental health.
- **Global Popularity**: In recent decades, mindfulness has gained immense popularity globally, becoming a mainstream practice for managing various aspects of life, including anxiety and stress.

Understanding the origins of mindfulness practices underscores their time-tested effectiveness and offers a glimpse into the wisdom of ancient traditions. While these practices have evolved and adapted over the years, their fundamental principles remain valuable tools for teenagers seeking relief from anxiety in today's fast-paced world.

Mindfulness vs. Meditation: Clarifying the Differences:

Learn how mindfulness differs from traditional meditation and why it's accessible to people of all backgrounds.

Mindfulness and meditation are terms often used interchangeably, but they refer to related yet distinct practices. Clarifying the differences between them can help individuals choose the approach that best suits their anxiety relief goals.

Mindfulness:

- **Definition**: Mindfulness again, is a mental practice focused on being fully present in the moment, observing thoughts, emotions, sensations, and the environment without judgment. It's about cultivating awareness and acceptance of whatever is happening right now.
- **Mindfulness in Daily Life**: Mindfulness can be integrated into daily activities, such as eating, walking, or breathing, allowing you to experience each moment with heightened awareness.
- **Informal Practice**: Mindfulness can be practiced informally, without setting aside specific time for meditation. It's about adopting a mindful attitude in everything you do.
- **Goal**: The primary goal of mindfulness is to develop a non-judgmental, accepting awareness of the present moment. It can reduce anxiety by helping individuals observe and respond to anxious thoughts and emotions with greater calm and clarity.

Meditation:

- **Definition**: Meditation is a structured mental practice that involves intentionally focusing the mind on a specific object, thought, or activity. It often requires a dedicated and quiet environment.
- **Formal Practice**: Meditation is typically practiced in a specific posture (e.g., sitting, lying down) and setting (e.g., a quiet room). It often follows a guided or unguided format, where attention is directed to a chosen point of focus.
- **Various Types**: There are various forms of meditation, including concentrative meditation (focused attention on one thing), loving-kindness meditation (cultivating feelings of compassion), and body scan meditation (systematic body awareness).
- **Goal**: The goals of meditation can vary depending on the type practiced. These may include improving concentration, increasing self-awareness, reducing stress, and promoting relaxation.

Relationship Between Mindfulness and Meditation:

- **Overlap**: Mindfulness practices can incorporate meditation as a tool for cultivating mindfulness. For example, focused attention on the breath (a common meditation technique) can be used to develop mindfulness.
- **Complementary**: Meditation and mindfulness are often used in tandem. While meditation offers structured training of the mind, mindfulness extends that awareness to everyday life.
- **Individual Preference**: Some individuals may prefer meditation as a formal practice, while others may find mindfulness integrated into their daily routines more accessible and sustainable.

Choosing the Right Approach for Anxiety Relief:

- **Mindfulness for Anxiety**: Mindfulness, with its emphasis on present-moment awareness and non-judgment, can be particularly effective for managing anxiety. It helps individuals observe anxious thoughts without getting entangled in them, fostering a sense of control and calm.
- **Meditation for Anxiety**: Meditation techniques can also be beneficial for anxiety relief by promoting relaxation and reducing stress. Concentrative meditation, in particular, can enhance focus and mental clarity, helping individuals manage anxious thoughts.

In summary, while mindfulness and meditation share common goals of promoting well-being and reducing anxiety, they differ in their formalities and approaches. The choice between them depends on personal preference and the specific needs and goals of the individual seeking anxiety relief. Some may find that a combination of both mindfulness and meditation provides a well-rounded approach to managing anxiety effectively.

The Essence of Being Present:

Understand the core principle of mindfulness—being fully present in the here and now—and how it can transform your life.

Being present, also known as "presence" or "present-moment awareness," is at the heart of mindfulness practice. It's a fundamental concept that lies at the core of anxiety relief through mindfulness.

The Definition of Being Present:
Being present means fully engaging with the current moment, giving it your undivided attention. It involves:

- **Awareness**: Paying attention to your thoughts, feelings, bodily sensations, and the environment as they unfold in real-time.

- **Acceptance**: Observing these experiences without judgment or the need to change them. It's about acknowledging whatever is happening without labeling it as good or bad.

- **Curiosity**: Approaching the present moment with an open and curious attitude, as if you're seeing, feeling, or experiencing things for the first time.

- **The Antidote to Overthinking**:
  Being present is a powerful antidote to overthinking—a common hallmark of anxiety. When you're fully present, you're not dwelling on the past or worrying about the future. Instead, you're grounded in the here and now.

- **Breaking the Cycle of Anxiety**:
  Anxiety often stems from ruminating about past regrets or anticipating future threats. Being present interrupts this cycle. By directing your focus to the present moment, you create a mental space where anxiety loses its grip.

- **Mindful Breathing as a Gateway**:
  Mindful breathing is one of the most accessible ways to practice being present. When you pay attention to your breath, you're focusing on something that is always in the present moment. As you inhale and exhale, you anchor yourself to the here and now.

- **Benefits of Being Present for Anxiety Relief**:
  - **Reduced Anxiety**: When you're present, you're not carried away by anxious thoughts or scenarios. You're less likely to get caught in a cycle of worry.
  - **Enhanced Emotional Regulation**: Being present allows you to observe your emotions as they arise without

reacting impulsively. This can lead to more measured and less emotionally charged responses to anxiety triggers.

- **Increased Self-Awareness**: The practice of being present fosters self-awareness. You gain insight into your thought patterns, emotional triggers, and physical responses to anxiety.
- **Greater Control**: By being present, you gain a sense of control over your reactions to anxiety-inducing situations. You can choose how to respond rather than react reflexively.

- **Challenges in Being Present**:
  - **Distractions**: In our fast-paced, digital world, distractions are abundant. Staying present can be challenging when there are constant demands on your attention.
  - **Habitual Thinking Patterns**: Breaking free from habitual thought patterns that lead to anxiety can take time and practice.
  - **Resistance**: Sometimes, people resist being present because they find discomfort in facing their thoughts and emotions directly. However, this discomfort can be an important part of growth and anxiety relief.

- **Mindfulness Techniques for Being Present**:
  - **Breath Awareness**: Focusing on your breath is an accessible way to practice being present. As you breathe in and out, you're in the present moment.
  - **Body Scan**: A body scan meditation involves mentally scanning your body from head to toe, paying attention to each part and any sensations you may feel.
  - **Grounding Exercises**: These involve using your senses, such as feeling the ground beneath your feet, to anchor yourself in the present moment.

Being present is a cornerstone of mindfulness practice and a transformative tool for managing anxiety. By cultivating this skill, teenagers can develop greater resilience, emotional well-being, and a sense of control over their anxiety-related challenges.

Section 2: Mindfulness Meditation Techniques

Mindfulness meditation is a powerful tool for developing mindfulness skills. This section introduces various meditation techniques:

- **Breath Awareness Meditation**: Explore the fundamental practice of focusing on the breath as a way to cultivate mindfulness and calm the mind.
- **Body Scan Meditation**: Learn how to scan your body for tension and sensations, promoting self-awareness and relaxation.
- **Loving-Kindness Meditation**: Discover a practice that nurtures feelings of compassion and goodwill, both for yourself and others.
- **Walking Meditation**: Explore a dynamic form of mindfulness that involves walking slowly and intentionally, connecting with each step.
- **Mindful Journaling**: Understand how journaling can be a form of mindfulness practice, helping you gain insights into your thoughts and emotions.

Mindfulness meditation techniques offer structured practices to cultivate mindfulness and reduce anxiety. Let's explore each of the five bullet points in detail:

1. Breath Awareness:

Definition: *Breath awareness meditation involves focusing your attention on your breath. It's one of the simplest yet most powerful mindfulness practices.*

How to Practice:

- Find a quiet and comfortable place to sit or lie down.
- Close your eyes if you're comfortable doing so.
- Direct your attention to your breath. Notice the sensation of the breath entering and leaving your nostrils or the rise and fall of your chest or abdomen.
- Whenever your mind wanders (which is perfectly normal), gently and without judgment, bring your focus back to your breath.
- Continue this process for a set period, whether it's a few minutes or longer.

Benefits for Anxiety Relief:

- Breath awareness meditation helps ground you in the present moment by focusing on the breath, reducing rumination about the past or future.
- It enhances self-awareness, allowing you to notice signs of anxiety in the body, such as shallow breathing or tension, so you can respond effectively.
- Regular practice can lead to a greater sense of calm and reduced anxiety over time.

2. Body Scan Meditation:

Definition: *Body scan meditation is a practice that involves systematically directing your attention to each part of your body, from head to toe. It's a practice of bodily awareness.*

How to Practice:

- Find a quiet and comfortable place to lie down.
- Close your eyes and take a few deep breaths to relax.
- Begin at the top of your head and slowly move your attention down your body.
- Notice any sensations or tension in each area without trying to change them.
- If you encounter tension, use your breath to release it as you exhale.
- Continue scanning your entire body, paying attention to each part.

Benefits for Anxiety Relief:

- Body scan meditation helps you develop a deeper connection to your body and its signals, which can be valuable for managing anxiety.
- It promotes relaxation and can alleviate physical tension associated with anxiety.

- By systematically scanning your body, you become more attuned to how anxiety manifests physically, allowing for early intervention.

3. Guided Visualization:

Definition: Guided visualization is a meditation practice that involves creating a mental image or scenario guided by a narrator's voice or your own imagination.

How to Practice:

- Find a comfortable place to sit or lie down.
- Close your eyes and take a few deep breaths to relax.
- Visualize a calming and peaceful place or scenario, such as a serene beach or a lush forest.
- Engage all your senses in the visualization. Notice the colors, sounds, textures, and even the scents in your mental image.
- Spend several minutes immersed in this calming mental landscape.

Benefits for Anxiety Relief:

- Guided visualization offers a break from anxious thoughts and a chance to immerse yourself in a positive and calming mental space.
- It reduces stress and induces relaxation, which can counteract the physiological symptoms of anxiety.
- Regular practice can provide a mental "escape" from the pressures and worries of daily life.

4. Loving-Kindness Meditation:

Definition: *Loving-kindness meditation, also known as metta meditation, is a practice of generating feelings of compassion, love, and goodwill towards oneself and others.*

How to Practice:

- Find a comfortable place to sit or lie down.
- Close your eyes and take a few deep breaths to center yourself.
- Begin by directing feelings of love and compassion towards yourself, repeating phrases like "May I be happy, may I be healthy, may I be at ease."
- Extend these feelings to loved ones, acquaintances, and even those with whom you have conflicts or difficulties.
- Continue repeating the phrases, adjusting them as needed, and allowing the feelings of loving-kindness to flow.

Benefits for Anxiety Relief:

- Loving-kindness meditation fosters self-compassion, which can counteract negative self-talk and self-criticism often associated with anxiety.
- It promotes a sense of connection and reduces feelings of isolation, which are common in anxiety.
- The practice of extending loving-kindness to difficult relationships can help ease interpersonal tensions and reduce social anxiety.

5. Mindfulness in Daily Life:

Definition: *Mindfulness in daily life means incorporating mindfulness into your everyday activities, such as eating, walking, or even washing dishes.*

How to Practice:

- Choose a daily activity to engage in mindfully. It could be as simple as eating a meal.
- As you engage in the chosen activity, focus your attention on the sensory experiences and sensations associated with it.

- For example, while eating mindfully, notice the colors, textures, and flavors of your food. Pay attention to the act of chewing and swallowing.
- Whenever your mind wanders to other thoughts, gently bring your focus back to the activity at hand.

Benefits for Anxiety Relief:

- Mindfulness in daily life allows you to anchor yourself in the present moment amidst the hustle and bustle of everyday tasks.
- It promotes awareness of your physical and emotional states, helping you recognize and respond to signs of anxiety as they arise.
- By integrating mindfulness into daily routines, you can maintain a more consistent practice and experience its cumulative benefits for anxiety relief.

Each of these mindfulness meditation techniques offers a unique approach to developing mindfulness and reducing anxiety. Experiment with these practices to discover which resonates most with you, and consider incorporating them into your daily routine for lasting anxiety relief.

Section 3: Mindfulness in Daily Life

The true power of mindfulness lies in its integration into daily life. In this section, we explore how to bring mindfulness into your everyday experiences:

- **Mindful Eating**: Learn how to savor each bite and cultivate a healthier relationship with food through mindful eating.
- **Mindful Communication**: Discover how to improve your relationships and deepen connections by practicing mindfulness in your interactions with others.
- **Mindfulness in Technology Use**: Understand the challenges posed by digital distractions and how to use mindfulness to regain control of your technology habits.
- **Cultivating Gratitude**: Explore the practice of gratitude and how it can shift your perspective, leading to greater contentment and positivity.

- **Mindfulness in Challenging Situations**: Learn how to apply mindfulness during stressful or difficult moments, helping you respond rather than react to life's challenges.

By the end of this chapter, you'll not only have a clear understanding of what mindfulness is but also practical tools and techniques to start your mindfulness journey and integrate it seamlessly into your daily life.

Integrating mindfulness into your daily life means making the practice a seamless part of your routine, allowing you to experience its benefits consistently. Let's delve deeper into each of the five bullet points in this section:

1. Mindful Eating:

Definition: *Mindful eating involves paying full attention to the act of eating, the sensory experiences of taste and texture, and the physical cues of hunger and fullness.*

How to Practice:

- Choose a meal or snacktime to practice mindful eating.
    - Eliminate distractions like phones or TV.
    - Examine your food with curiosity. Notice its colors, shapes, and textures.
    - Take small bites and savor each one. Pay attention to the flavors, aromas, and the sensation of chewing and swallowing.
    - Pause occasionally to check in with your body's hunger and fullness cues.

Benefits for Anxiety Relief:

- Mindful eating can reduce emotional eating by helping you become more attuned to physical hunger and fullness signals.
    - It fosters a healthier relationship with food, reducing anxiety related to body image and dieting.
    - By slowing down and savoring each bite, you can experience greater enjoyment in eating and reduce stress associated with rushed meals.

2. Mindful Walking:

Definition: *Mindful walking is a practice of walking with awareness and intention, focusing on each step and the sensations associated with it.*

How to Practice:

- Find a quiet and safe place to walk, whether it's indoors or outdoors.
  - Begin walking at a slower pace than usual.
  - Pay attention to the sensation of your feet lifting, moving, and landing with each step.
  - Observe the feeling of your body in motion and the connection between your feet and the ground.
  - Stay present in the experience, letting go of distractions and racing thoughts.

Benefits for Anxiety Relief:

- Mindful walking can be a moving meditation, offering a break from anxious thoughts and a chance to connect with the world around you.
  - It promotes a sense of grounding and stability, which can be especially helpful during anxious moments.
  - The rhythmic nature of walking can induce a calming effect and reduce stress.

3. Mindful Breathing:

Definition: *Mindful breathing involves incorporating short moments of mindfulness into your day by paying attention to your breath.*

How to Practice:

- Throughout the day, take short breaks to focus on your breath.
  - It can be as simple as pausing for a few seconds during a busy day to take a few deep breaths.
  - Direct your attention to the sensation of your breath entering and leaving your nostrils or the rise and fall of your abdomen.

- ■ Use these moments to ground yourself in the present and let go of tension.

Benefits for Anxiety Relief:

- ○ Mindful breathing can serve as an anchor, helping you return to the present moment when anxiety threatens to pull you into rumination or worry.
  - ■ It provides a quick and effective tool for managing stress and anxiety, even in the midst of a hectic schedule.
  - ■ Over time, these short moments of mindfulness can accumulate, fostering an ongoing sense of calm and resilience.

4. Mindful Communication:

Definition: *Mindful communication is the practice of being fully present and attentive during conversations, both as a speaker and a listener.*

How to Practice:

- ○ When engaging in conversations, especially important ones, make a conscious effort to be fully present.
  - ■ Give your full attention to the speaker, maintaining eye contact and avoiding distractions like phones or multitasking.
  - ■ Listen actively, without interrupting or planning your response in advance.
  - ■ Pause before responding, allowing space for thoughtful and considerate replies.

Benefits for Anxiety Relief:

- ○ Mindful communication can reduce social anxiety by promoting genuine connection and reducing self-consciousness.
    - It fosters better understanding in relationships and can reduce misunderstandings or conflicts that may contribute to anxiety.
    - By being fully present in conversations, you can experience a sense of connection and ease in social interactions.

5. Mindfulness in Routine Activities:

Definition: *Mindfulness in routine activities means approaching everyday tasks with awareness and intention, such as brushing your teeth, doing dishes, or even commuting.*

How to Practice:

- ○ Choose one routine activity to start with, such as washing dishes.
    - While engaging in the activity, focus on the sensory experiences, sensations, and movements involved.
    - Notice the temperature of the water, the texture of the dishes, and the repetitive actions.
    - If your mind wanders, gently bring your attention back to the activity.

Benefits for Anxiety Relief:

- ○ Mindfulness in routine activities transforms mundane tasks into opportunities for relaxation and presence, reducing anxiety.
    - It encourages a sense of gratitude and appreciation for the simple moments in life, which can counteract the stress of daily demands.
    - By incorporating mindfulness into routine activities, you can build a consistent mindfulness practice that fits seamlessly into your daily life.

These mindfulness practices in daily life offer accessible ways to incorporate mindfulness into your routine, promoting a sense of calm, presence, and anxiety relief amidst the busyness of everyday life.

Chapter 7: Breathing Techniques for Calm

Breath is more than just a physiological function; it's a bridge between mind and body, a source of calm, and a tool for managing anxiety. In this chapter, we explore the importance of breath, breathing exercises tailored to combat anxiety, and how to seamlessly incorporate breathwork into your daily routine.

Section 1: The Importance of Breath

The breath is an often-overlooked ally in managing anxiety. This section delves into the significance of understanding and harnessing the power of breath:

- **The Mind-Body Connection**: Explore how breath serves as a link between your mental and physical states, influencing your emotions and well-being.
- **Breath as an Anchor**: Understand how the breath can be an anchor in turbulent times, providing stability and grounding when anxiety threatens to overwhelm.
- **Breathing and the Autonomic Nervous System**: Discover the role of breath in regulating the autonomic nervous system, affecting your body's stress response and relaxation mechanisms.
- **Breath Awareness**: Learn how the simple act of paying attention to your breath can bring awareness to the present moment and reduce anxiety.

Breath is central to mindfulness and anxiety relief. Understanding the significance of breath goes beyond its biological function; it's about recognizing its role in calming the mind and body. Understanding the mind-body connection, particularly in the context of breath, is vital for managing anxiety effectively. Let's explore each of the four bullet points in this section in more detail:

1. The Mind-Body Connection:

Definition: *The mind-body connection refers to the intricate relationship between your mental and emotional state (mind) and your physical state (body). It highlights how changes in one can influence the other.*

- **Anxiety as a Mind-Body Experience:** Anxiety is a prime example of the mind-body connection in action. When you experience anxiety, it's not limited to your thoughts and emotions; it manifests physically as well. You might notice symptoms such as increased heart rate, muscle tension, sweaty palms, and rapid breathing.
- **Two-Way Communication:** The mind and body communicate bidirectionally. Your thoughts and emotions can trigger physical responses, and conversely, physical sensations and changes can affect your thoughts and emotions. This interplay can either exacerbate anxiety or be harnessed to reduce it.
- **Implications for Anxiety Management:** Recognizing the mind-body connection in anxiety management empowers you to address anxiety from both angles. While you can work on changing anxious thought patterns, you can also employ techniques to influence your physical responses, such as breathwork, to bring about a sense of calm and relaxation.

2. Breath as an Anchor:

Definition: *Using the breath as an anchor refers to the practice of focusing your attention on your breath as a way to stay grounded in the present moment.*

- The Role of the Anchor: In mindfulness and breathwork, the breath serves as an anchor that helps you tether your awareness to the present. When you focus on your breath, you divert your attention away from anxious thoughts about the past or future and ground yourself in the here and now.
- Staying Present: Anchoring to your breath allows you to stay present, which is a powerful antidote to anxiety. Anxiety often arises when your mind becomes entangled in worries about what might happen or regrets about what has already occurred. By returning your focus to your breath, you step out of that cycle.
- Enhanced Self-Regulation: The breath as an anchor supports self-regulation. It helps you become more aware of your thoughts and emotions without being overwhelmed by them. This awareness allows you to respond to anxiety in a more

measured and controlled way.

3. Breathing and the Autonomic Nervous System:

Definition: *The autonomic nervous system (ANS) is the part of your nervous system responsible for regulating involuntary bodily functions, including heart rate, digestion, and respiratory rate. It has two primary branches: the sympathetic (fight-or-flight) and parasympathetic (rest and digest) nervous systems.*

- **Sympathetic Response and Anxiety:** When anxiety triggers the fight-or-flight response, the sympathetic nervous system becomes dominant. This leads to physiological changes like increased heart rate, shallow breathing, and heightened alertness—responses aimed at preparing the body to face a perceived threat.
- **Parasympathetic Response and Calm**: On the other hand, the parasympathetic nervous system is associated with relaxation and recovery. It promotes slower heart rate, deeper breathing, and a sense of calm.
- **Breath's Role in Shifting the ANS:** Your breath acts as a lever for influencing the ANS. Conscious, deep breathing techniques can shift the body from a sympathetic-dominant state to a parasympathetic-dominant state, promoting relaxation and reducing anxiety.

4. Breath Awareness:

Definition: *Breath awareness is the practice of paying deliberate attention to your breath, observing its rhythm, depth, and sensations.*

- **The Power of Observation:** When you become aware of your breath, you are observing it without judgment or the need to change it. This observational stance is central to mindfulness and allows you to notice your breath's natural patterns.
- **The Gateway to Mindfulness:** Breath awareness is often a gateway to broader mindfulness practices. It teaches you how to direct your attention, notice thoughts without getting caught up

in them, and cultivate a non-judgmental awareness of the present moment.

- **Enhancing Breath Control:** By becoming more aware of your breath, you gain better control over it. This control is valuable for managing anxiety because you can intentionally slow your breathing, deepen it, and bring about a sense of calm when needed.

Understanding the mind-body connection, the role of the breath as an anchor, its influence on the autonomic nervous system, and the practice of breath awareness equips you with valuable insights and techniques for managing anxiety effectively. By harnessing the power of your breath, you can transform the way you respond to anxiety and cultivate a greater sense of calm and control.

Section 2: Breathing Exercises for Anxiety

Breathing exercises are powerful tools for anxiety relief. This section provides a practical guide to specific techniques:

- **Diaphragmatic Breathing**: Master the art of diaphragmatic breathing, a foundational technique that promotes relaxation and reduces anxiety.
- **4-7-8 Breathing**: Explore the 4-7-8 technique, a simple yet effective breathing exercise that calms the nervous system and induces a sense of tranquility.
- **Box Breathing**: Understand the concept of box breathing, a method that involves equal counts for inhaling, holding, exhaling, and resting, allowing for profound relaxation.
- **Alternate Nostril Breathing**: Discover alternate nostril breathing, a yogic practice that balances the left and right sides of the brain, fostering mental equilibrium.
- **Mindful Breathing**: Learn how to combine mindfulness with breathwork, using the breath to anchor your awareness in the present moment and alleviate anxiety.

Incorporating breathwork into your daily routine is a powerful way to harness the benefits of mindful breathing for anxiety relief. Let's explore each of the four bullets in this section in more detail:

Breathing exercises are valuable tools for managing anxiety. In this section, we'll explore five different breathing techniques, each with its unique approach and benefits:

1. Diaphragmatic Breathing:

Definition: *Diaphragmatic breathing, also known as abdominal or deep breathing, focuses on using the diaphragm—a dome-shaped muscle located below the lungs—to draw air into the lower part of the lungs.*

- **How to Practice:**
    - Sit or lie down comfortably.
    - Place one hand on your chest and the other on your abdomen.
    - Inhale slowly through your nose, allowing your abdomen to rise as you fill your lungs.
    - Exhale slowly through your mouth, feeling your abdomen fall.
    - Continue this process for several minutes, maintaining a steady and relaxed rhythm.

- **Benefits for Anxiety Relief:**
    - Diaphragmatic breathing encourages slow, deep breaths, which can counteract the shallow, rapid breathing associated with anxiety.
    - It helps activate the body's relaxation response, reducing the physiological symptoms of anxiety, such as increased heart rate and muscle tension.

- Practicing diaphragmatic breathing regularly can enhance your overall lung capacity and improve oxygen exchange, contributing to better overall health.

2. 4-7-8 Breathing:

Definition: *The 4-7-8 breathing technique is a specific breath pattern designed to induce relaxation and alleviate anxiety.*

- **How to Practice:**
    - Sit or lie down in a comfortable position.
    - Close your eyes and take a deep breath in through your nose for a count of four.
    - Hold your breath for a count of seven.
    - Exhale slowly and audibly through your mouth for a count of eight.
    - Repeat this cycle for several rounds, gradually extending the counts if comfortable.

- **Benefits for Anxiety Relief:**
    - The 4-7-8 pattern helps regulate your breath, slowing it down and promoting a sense of calm.
    - The extended exhale activates the parasympathetic nervous system, reducing stress and anxiety.
    - Practicing 4-7-8 breathing before bed can enhance sleep quality by promoting relaxation.

3. Box Breathing:

Definition: *Box breathing is a breathwork technique that emphasizes equalizing the duration of inhales, exhales, and pauses.*

- **How to Practice:**
    - Sit or stand comfortably.
    - Inhale through your nose for a count of four.
    - Hold your breath for a count of four.
    - Exhale through your mouth for a count of four.

- Pause for a count of four before beginning the cycle again.

- **Benefits for Anxiety Relief:**
    - Box breathing promotes balance in your breath and activates the relaxation response.
    - It provides a structured and easily remembered technique for managing anxiety in real-time, even during stressful situations.
    - Box breathing can be discreetly practiced in various settings, making it a versatile tool for anxiety management.

4. Alternate Nostril Breathing:

Definition: *Alternate nostril breathing, or Nadi Shodhana in yoga, involves alternating the flow of breath through each nostril to balance the body's energy.*

- **How to Practice:**
    - Sit comfortably with your spine erect.
    - Close your right nostril with your right thumb and inhale deeply through your left nostril.
    - Close your left nostril with your right ring finger, release your right nostril, and exhale through the right nostril.
    - Inhale deeply through the right nostril.
    - Close your right nostril again, release your left nostril, and exhale through the left nostril.
    - Repeat this cycle for several rounds.

- **Benefits for Anxiety Relief:**
    - Alternate nostril breathing balances the left and right hemispheres of the brain, promoting mental clarity and emotional balance.
    - It can alleviate symptoms of anxiety by calming the mind and reducing stress.

- This technique is particularly useful for moments when you need to regain focus and composure.

5. Mindful Breathing:

Definition: *Mindful breathing involves simply paying attention to your breath, observing its natural rhythm without attempting to change it.*

- **How to Practice:**
    - Find a quiet and comfortable place to sit or lie down.
    - Close your eyes and bring your awareness to your breath.
    - Notice the sensation of the breath as it enters and leaves your nostrils or the rise and fall of your abdomen.
    - If your mind wanders, gently bring your attention back to your breath without judgment.

- **Benefits for Anxiety Relief:**
    - Mindful breathing is a fundamental practice in mindfulness, which encourages non-judgmental awareness of the present moment.
    - It helps you become more attuned to your thoughts and emotions, fostering emotional regulation.
    - Mindful breathing can be practiced at any time, serving as an anchor to the present moment and a tool for managing anxiety and stress as it arises.

Each of these breathing techniques offers a unique approach to managing anxiety and promoting relaxation. By incorporating these practices into your daily routine, you can develop a versatile toolkit for managing anxiety and enhancing your overall well-being.

Section 3: Incorporating Breathwork into Daily Routine

Breathwork is most effective when it becomes a seamless part of your daily life. In this section, we explore how to integrate breathwork into your routines:

- **Morning Breath Rituals**: Explore ways to start your day mindfully, setting a positive tone for the hours ahead through intentional breathwork.
- **Breath Breaks**: Learn how to take short, mindful breath breaks throughout the day to reduce stress and maintain a calm, centered mindset.
- **Breathwork for Sleep**: Discover techniques to calm the mind and prepare for restful sleep, ensuring that breathwork aids in achieving a good night's sleep.
- **Breathwork as a Stress Response**: Understand how to use breathwork as a response to stressful situations, helping you stay composed and focused in the face of challenges.

By the end of this chapter, you'll have a deep appreciation for the role of breath in managing anxiety, a repertoire of effective breathing exercises, and the knowledge to seamlessly incorporate breathwork into your daily routines, empowering you to navigate life's challenges with greater ease and calmness.

1. Morning Breath Rituals:

Definition: *Morning breath rituals involve starting your day with intentional breathwork practices to set a positive tone and enhance your overall well-being.*

- **Setting the Tone**: The way you begin your day can significantly impact your mindset and emotional state. Incorporating breathwork into your morning routine can set a calm and centered tone for the day ahead.

- **Types of Morning Breath Rituals:**
    - Deep Breathing: Dedicate a few minutes to deep, diaphragmatic breathing. Inhale slowly through your

nose, allowing your abdomen to rise, and exhale slowly through your mouth, feeling your abdomen fall.
- Morning Meditation: Combine breath awareness with meditation. Sit quietly and focus on your breath, allowing thoughts to come and go without attachment.
- Positive Affirmations: While breathing mindfully, recite positive affirmations to cultivate a positive mindset for the day.

- **Benefits for Anxiety Relief:** Morning breath rituals can reduce morning anxiety and help you approach your day with a sense of calm and focus. They provide a buffer against stress and anxiety that may arise during the day.

2. Breath Breaks:

Definition: *Breath breaks are short, intentional moments throughout your day when you pause to engage in brief breathwork exercises.*

- **Stress Reduction:** Incorporating breath breaks into your daily routine serves as a proactive strategy for stress reduction. Rather than waiting until anxiety intensifies, you take preventive measures by engaging in short, calming breathwork exercises.

- **Types of Breath Breaks:**
  - Minute Breathing: Take one-minute breath breaks during transitions or whenever you feel stress building. Inhale deeply for a count of four, hold for a count of four, exhale for a count of four, and hold for a count of four before resuming your tasks.
  - Focused Breathing: When faced with challenging situations or overwhelming emotions, step aside for a brief breath break. Focus on your breath to regain composure and clarity.
  - Office Chair Breathing: If you're in a work or school environment, practice deep breathing while sitting in your chair. This discreet technique can help you manage stress in real-time.

- **Benefits for Anxiety Relief:** Breath breaks provide you with on-the-spot tools to manage stress and anxiety. They offer quick relief, enhance your emotional resilience, and help you stay present during challenging moments.

3. Breathwork for Sleep:

Definition: *Breathwork for sleep involves using specific breathwork techniques to improve the quality of your sleep and promote relaxation before bedtime.*

- **Sleep Hygiene:** Sleep is crucial for managing anxiety, and incorporating breathwork into your bedtime routine can enhance your sleep hygiene. Sleep hygiene refers to practices that promote restful and rejuvenating sleep.

- **Types of Breathwork for Sleep:**
    - 4-7-8 Breathing: Practice the 4-7-8 breathing technique mentioned earlier before going to bed. This can help calm your nervous system and prepare your body for sleep.
    - Progressive Relaxation: Combine breathwork with progressive muscle relaxation. As you inhale, tense a specific muscle group, and as you exhale, release the tension. This relaxation technique can prepare your body for sleep.
    - Visualization and Breath: Combine deep breathing with a calming mental visualization, such as picturing a peaceful place. As you inhale, imagine yourself breathing in tranquility, and as you exhale, release any tension or stress.

- **Benefits for Anxiety Relief:** Breathwork for sleep can alleviate anxiety-related sleep disturbances, such as racing thoughts and restlessness. It promotes relaxation and a sense of calm, facilitating more restorative sleep.

4. Breathwork as a Stress Response:

Definition: *Using breathwork as a stress response involves recognizing when you're experiencing stress or anxiety and proactively engaging in breathwork to counteract these responses.*

- **Early Intervention:** One of the advantages of incorporating breathwork into your daily routine is that it allows for early intervention. Instead of waiting until stress or anxiety escalates, you can recognize the initial signs and employ breathwork to manage them.

- **Benefits for Anxiety Relief:** By using breathwork as a stress response, you equip yourself with a proactive tool for managing anxiety. It prevents stress from escalating into more severe anxiety and promotes emotional resilience. Regular practice can lead to a reduced overall stress level and greater control over anxious responses.

Incorporating breathwork into your daily routine through morning breath rituals, breath breaks, breathwork for sleep, and using breathwork as a stress response empowers you to manage anxiety actively and promote emotional well-being. These practices enhance your ability to stay grounded, reduce stress, and respond to anxiety with greater resilience and control.

Chapter 8: Cognitive Behavioral Therapy (CBT) for Teens

Cognitive-Behavioral Therapy (CBT) is a powerful psychological approach that can help teenagers identify and reframe negative thought patterns, ultimately reducing anxiety. In this chapter, we explore the foundations of CBT, the process of identifying negative thought patterns, and practical exercises and strategies for implementing CBT techniques.

Section 1: How CBT Works

CBT is a structured, goal-oriented therapy that focuses on the connection between thoughts, feelings, and behaviors. This section provides an overview of the key principles of CBT:

- **Understanding the Cognitive Triad**: Learn how thoughts, emotions, and behaviors are interconnected and how altering one component can influence the others.
- **Challenging Core Beliefs**: Explore the process of identifying and challenging core beliefs or automatic thoughts that contribute to anxiety.
- **The Role of Cognitive Restructuring**: Understand how cognitive restructuring techniques are used to replace negative thought patterns with more constructive and realistic ones.
- **Behavioral Experiments**: Discover how CBT encourages the use of behavioral experiments to test and modify the beliefs that underlie anxiety.

Understanding the cognitive triad is essential for comprehending the core principles of Cognitive-Behavioral Therapy (CBT). Let's delve into each of the four bullet points in this section:

Understanding the Cognitive Triad:

Definition: *The cognitive triad is a foundational concept in CBT. It refers to the three categories of negative beliefs that individuals with anxiety often hold about themselves, their future, and the world around them.*

The Three Components:
- Negative Self-View: This component involves negative beliefs about oneself. For instance, individuals with anxiety may believe they are inadequate, unlovable, or incapable of coping with challenges.
- Negative Worldview: This component pertains to negative beliefs about the world. It includes thoughts that the world is a dangerous or hostile place, and that bad things are likely to happen.
- Negative Future Orientation: Here, individuals with anxiety anticipate negative outcomes in the future. They often expect the worst-case scenario and may fear that things will never improve.

Impact on Anxiety: The cognitive triad contributes to the perpetuation of anxiety. These negative beliefs can lead to rumination, excessive worrying, and avoidance behaviors. By addressing and modifying these beliefs, CBT aims to alleviate anxiety symptoms.

Challenging Core Beliefs:

Definition: *Challenging core beliefs involves questioning and reevaluating the negative and irrational beliefs that make up the cognitive triad.*

- **Identifying Core Beliefs:** Through CBT, individuals learn to identify their core beliefs by paying attention to their thoughts and emotions during anxious episodes. They recognize the patterns of negative thinking that contribute to anxiety.
- **Cognitive Distortions:** Core beliefs often involve cognitive distortions, such as all-or-nothing thinking, catastrophizing, and overgeneralization. CBT helps individuals recognize these

distortions and replace them with more balanced and rational beliefs.

- **Techniques for Challenging Core Beliefs:** Therapists and individuals work together to challenge core beliefs through various techniques, including:
- **Socratic Questioning:** This involves asking probing questions to explore the evidence for and against a particular belief.
- **Behavioral Experiments:** Conducting experiments to test the validity of a belief.
- **Reframing:** Viewing situations from different perspectives to develop a more balanced outlook.

The Role of Cognitive Restructuring:

Definition: *Cognitive restructuring is a central component of CBT. It refers to the process of identifying and changing irrational or negative thought patterns.*

- **Steps in Cognitive Restructuring:**
    - Identify Negative Thoughts: The first step is to become aware of negative thoughts, especially those related to anxiety.
    - Evaluate Thoughts: Individuals learn to evaluate the accuracy and validity of their thoughts. They ask questions like, "Is this thought based on facts or assumptions?"
    - Challenge and Replace: Negative thoughts are challenged and replaced with more balanced and rational alternatives. This step often involves generating evidence that supports a more constructive belief.
    - Practice: Cognitive restructuring is an ongoing process. Individuals practice these steps regularly to develop healthier thought patterns.

- **Benefits for Anxiety Relief:** Cognitive restructuring empowers individuals to gain control over their thought processes. It helps them break free from the cycle of negative thinking that fuels anxiety and replace it with more constructive thought patterns.

Behavioral Experiments:

Definition: *Behavioral experiments are a practical aspect of CBT that involves testing the validity of anxious beliefs through real-life experiences.*

- **How They Work:** In a behavioral experiment, individuals work with their therapist to design and carry out an activity or experiment that challenges their anxious beliefs. The goal is to gather evidence to support more realistic and balanced thinking.

- **Examples of Behavioral Experiments:**
    - If someone has a fear of social situations, they may gradually expose themselves to social gatherings, keeping track of their experiences and feelings.
    - For someone with health-related anxiety, they might work on reducing avoidance behaviors by visiting a doctor to discuss their concerns.

- **Benefits for Anxiety Relief:** Behavioral experiments provide tangible proof that challenges irrational beliefs. As individuals confront their fears and test their assumptions, they often discover that their anxiety is based on unfounded or exaggerated concerns. This process can lead to reduced anxiety and increased confidence.

Understanding the cognitive triad, challenging core beliefs, practicing cognitive restructuring, and engaging in behavioral experiments are fundamental components of CBT. By addressing these aspects, individuals with anxiety can learn to reframe their thinking, break free from negative thought patterns, and reduce the impact of anxiety on their lives.

Section 2: Identifying Negative Thought Patterns

Before you can change negative thought patterns, you must first identify them. This section delves into techniques for recognizing and understanding these patterns:

- **Self-Monitoring**: Learn how to keep a thought diary or journal to track and record your thoughts and feelings, enabling you to identify recurring negative patterns.

- **Cognitive Distortions**: Explore common cognitive distortions, such as black-and-white thinking, catastrophizing, and personalization, and how they contribute to anxiety.
- **Recognizing Automatic Thoughts**: Understand the concept of automatic thoughts—spontaneous, often subconscious, thoughts that can lead to anxiety and distress.
- **Identifying Core Beliefs**: Discover how to uncover deep-seated core beliefs that drive anxiety, often formed during childhood or past experiences.

Identifying negative thought patterns is a crucial step in Cognitive-Behavioral Therapy (CBT) for managing anxiety. Let's explore each of the four bullet points in this section in greater detail:

Self-Monitoring:

Definition: *Self-monitoring involves observing and recording your thoughts, emotions, and behaviors as they relate to anxiety-inducing situations or triggers.*

- **The Role of Self-Monitoring:** Self-monitoring is the foundation of CBT because it provides insight into the patterns and triggers of anxiety. It helps individuals become more aware of their internal experiences and how they relate to anxiety symptoms.

- **Self-Monitoring Techniques:** Therapists often encourage individuals to maintain an anxiety journal or use smartphone apps to record their thoughts, emotions, and behaviors. This can be especially helpful when identifying patterns and triggers that contribute to anxiety.

- **Benefits for Anxiety Relief**: Self-monitoring allows individuals to:
  - Recognize recurring thought patterns and cognitive distortions that fuel anxiety.
  - Gain insight into the specific situations or contexts that trigger anxiety.
  - Track progress over time as they implement CBT techniques.

Cognitive Distortions:

Definition: *Cognitive distortions, also known as thinking errors or irrational beliefs, are patterns of thinking that are inaccurate and tend to reinforce negative emotions, including anxiety.*

- **Common Cognitive Distortions:** There are several common cognitive distortions, including:
    - All-or-Nothing Thinking: Viewing situations in extreme, black-and-white terms.
    - Catastrophizing: Expecting the worst possible outcome.
    - Overgeneralization: Making broad, negative conclusions based on limited evidence.
    - Personalization: Blaming oneself for external events or circumstances.

- **Recognizing Cognitive Distortions**: CBT helps individuals recognize these cognitive distortions by teaching them to question their thoughts. Instead of accepting negative thoughts at face value, individuals learn to assess their accuracy and validity.

- **Benefits for Anxiety Relief:** Identifying and challenging cognitive distortions is a pivotal step in reducing anxiety. By recognizing and correcting distorted thinking, individuals can replace irrational beliefs with more balanced and rational thoughts, leading to reduced anxiety and improved emotional well-being.

Recognizing Automatic Thoughts:

Definition: *Automatic thoughts are the rapid, often subconscious, thoughts that occur in response to situations or triggers. These thoughts are typically automatic and can contribute to anxiety.*

- **The Nature of Automatic Thoughts:** Automatic thoughts are spontaneous and tend to be emotionally charged. They are the initial reactions to a situation and often reflect cognitive distortions.

- **Recognizing Automatic Thoughts:** In CBT, individuals learn to become more aware of their automatic thoughts by:
    - Paying attention to the thoughts that arise when they feel anxious or distressed.
    - Identifying thought patterns associated with specific triggers or situations.
    - Using self-monitoring techniques to record automatic thoughts.

- **Benefits for Anxiety Relief:** Recognizing automatic thoughts is the first step in challenging and modifying them. By becoming aware of these initial reactions, individuals can interrupt the anxiety cycle and replace automatic negative thoughts with more constructive ones.

Identifying Core Beliefs:

Definition: *Core beliefs are deeply ingrained, fundamental beliefs about oneself, others, and the world. These beliefs are often formed in childhood and can play a significant role in anxiety.*

- **Importance of Identifying Core Beliefs:** Core beliefs underlie automatic thoughts and cognitive distortions. Identifying and understanding these core beliefs is essential for addressing the root causes of anxiety.

- **The Role of Therapist:** Therapists in CBT work with individuals to uncover core beliefs through dialogue, exploration, and guided questioning. Identifying these beliefs often requires a therapeutic relationship and a safe space for individuals to express their thoughts and emotions.

- **Benefits for Anxiety Relief:** Once core beliefs are identified, individuals can work with their therapist to challenge and reframe them. By altering these deeply ingrained beliefs, individuals can experience profound and lasting changes in their thought patterns and anxiety levels.

Identifying negative thought patterns, including self-monitoring, recognizing cognitive distortions, becoming aware of automatic thoughts, and uncovering core beliefs, are critical steps in the CBT process. These steps pave the way for individuals to gain insight into the roots of their anxiety and develop strategies for managing and ultimately reducing its impact on their lives.

Section 3: Practical Exercises and Strategies

This section provides actionable exercises and strategies for implementing CBT techniques in your daily life:

- **Cognitive Restructuring**: Step-by-step guidance on how to challenge and reframe negative thoughts, replacing them with more rational and balanced ones.
- **Exposure Therapy**: Learn how gradual exposure to anxiety-provoking situations can reduce fear and anxiety over time, with specific strategies for implementation.
- **Relaxation Techniques**: Explore relaxation exercises, such as deep breathing, progressive muscle relaxation, and mindfulness, to manage anxiety symptoms.
- **Homework Assignments**: Understand the importance of homework assignments in CBT and how they reinforce the skills learned in therapy sessions.
- **Building a Support System**: Discover the role of social support in CBT and how involving family or friends can enhance the effectiveness of the therapy.

By the end of this chapter, you will have a comprehensive understanding of how CBT works, the ability to identify negative thought patterns that contribute to anxiety, and a toolkit of practical exercises and strategies to begin applying CBT techniques in your daily life, promoting lasting change and emotional well-being.

This section outlines practical exercises and strategies commonly used in Cognitive-Behavioral Therapy (CBT) to manage anxiety. Let's explore each of the five bullet points in this section in greater detail:

Cognitive Restructuring:

Definition: *Cognitive restructuring is a core technique in CBT that involves identifying and challenging irrational or negative thought patterns to replace them with more balanced and rational beliefs.*

- **How It Works:** Individuals learn to recognize their automatic negative thoughts and cognitive distortions, such as catastrophizing or all-or-nothing thinking. Through guided exercises with a therapist or on their own, they reevaluate these thoughts for accuracy and validity.

- **Benefits for Anxiety Relief:** Cognitive restructuring helps individuals develop healthier thought patterns and beliefs, reducing the intensity and frequency of anxious thoughts. It empowers them to view situations more objectively and less emotionally, leading to reduced anxiety and improved emotional well-being.

Exposure Therapy:

Definition: *Exposure therapy is a technique used to confront and gradually desensitize individuals to anxiety-inducing situations or triggers.*

- **How It Works:** In exposure therapy, individuals are systematically exposed to their anxiety triggers in a controlled and gradual manner. This exposure helps them confront their fears and anxieties, allowing them to become less sensitive to the triggers over time.

- **Types of Exposure:** There are two primary types of exposure therapy:
    - In vivo exposure: Real-life exposure to feared situations.
    - Imaginal exposure: Confronting feared situations through vivid imagination.

- **Benefits for Anxiety Relief:** Exposure therapy helps individuals build resilience against their anxiety triggers. Over time, repeated exposure leads to habituation, where the anxiety response diminishes. This technique can be particularly effective for specific phobias and anxiety disorders like post-traumatic stress disorder (PTSD).

Relaxation Techniques:

Definition: *Relaxation techniques are exercises and practices designed to promote physical and mental relaxation, reducing anxiety symptoms.*

- **Common Relaxation Techniques:**
    - Deep Breathing: Encourages slow, deep breaths to calm the nervous system.
    - Progressive Muscle Relaxation: Involves tensing and relaxing muscle groups to release physical tension.
    - Guided Imagery: Uses mental imagery to create a calming, peaceful mental state.
    - Mindfulness Meditation: Promotes non-judgmental awareness of the present moment.
    - Yoga: Combines physical postures, breathwork, and meditation to promote relaxation.

- **Benefits for Anxiety Relief:** Relaxation techniques provide individuals with practical tools to manage anxiety symptoms in real-time. These techniques can reduce muscle tension, lower heart rate, and create a sense of calm, helping individuals regain control over their anxiety.

Homework Assignments:

Definition: *Homework assignments are tasks and exercises assigned by therapists for individuals to complete between therapy sessions.*

- **Purpose:** Homework assignments reinforce the skills learned in therapy sessions and encourage individuals to apply these skills in their daily lives. They promote consistent practice and skill development.

- **Types of Homework Assignments:** These can include keeping thought records to monitor automatic thoughts, practicing relaxation techniques, engaging in exposure exercises, and completing cognitive restructuring exercises.

- **Benefits for Anxiety Relief:** Homework assignments extend the therapeutic process beyond the therapist's office. They empower individuals to take an active role in their treatment, apply CBT techniques, and track their progress. This promotes a sense of agency and self-efficacy in managing anxiety.

Building a Support System:

Definition: *Building a support system involves identifying and nurturing relationships with individuals who can provide emotional support, encouragement, and understanding.*

- **The Role of a Support System:** A strong support system can provide individuals with a safety net during difficult times, reduce feelings of isolation, and offer a source of motivation and accountability.
- **Types of Support:** Support can come from various sources, including family members, friends, support groups, or online communities.
- **Benefits for Anxiety Relief:** A robust support system can help individuals cope with anxiety more effectively. Supportive relationships provide opportunities to share experiences, receive validation, and practice newly acquired CBT skills in real-life situations.

By incorporating these practical exercises and strategies into their lives, individuals undergoing CBT for anxiety can develop a comprehensive toolkit for managing their symptoms. These techniques empower them to challenge and reframe negative thoughts, confront anxiety triggers, promote relaxation, track their progress, and access emotional support, leading to improved overall well-being and reduced anxiety.

Chapter 9: Healthy Lifestyle Choices

A healthy lifestyle is a cornerstone of managing anxiety effectively. This chapter explores the vital role of diet and nutrition, the benefits of exercise and physical activity, and the importance of establishing good sleep hygiene in nurturing both mental and physical well-being.

Section 1: Diet and Nutrition

A balanced diet plays a significant role in maintaining mental health and managing anxiety. In this section, we delve into the importance of mindful eating and nutritional choices:

- **Mindful Eating**: Understand the practice of mindful eating, which encourages you to savor each bite, eat with awareness, and build a healthier relationship with food.
- **The Gut-Brain Connection**: Explore the emerging science of the gut-brain connection, which suggests that the health of your gut can influence your mental well-being.
- **Nutritional Considerations**: Learn about key nutrients, vitamins, and minerals that play a role in anxiety management and how to incorporate them into your diet.
- **Balanced Eating**: Discover the significance of balanced meals, regular eating patterns, and the impact of blood sugar levels on mood and anxiety.

In this section, we'll delve deeper into the concepts of mindful eating, the gut-brain connection, and nutritional considerations, including balanced eating, and their role in managing anxiety:

Mindful Eating:

Mindful Eating Defined: *Mindful eating is a practice rooted in mindfulness, encouraging individuals to cultivate awareness and presence during meals. It goes* *beyond the act of consuming food; it's about experiencing each bite fully, engaging the senses, and being attuned to physical and emotional cues related to eating.*

- **The Practice of Mindful Eating:**
    - Slowing Down: Mindful eating encourages a slower pace of eating. It involves savoring each bite, chewing thoroughly, and being present with the sensations of taste and texture.
    - Emotional Awareness: This approach fosters an understanding of emotional triggers for eating. It encourages individuals to distinguish between physical hunger and emotional hunger, reducing impulsive eating in response to stress or anxiety.
    - Mindful Choices: It emphasizes making mindful choices about food selection, considering both nutritional value and personal preferences.

- **Benefits for Anxiety Relief**: Mindful eating can be a powerful tool for anxiety management:
    - It helps individuals break the cycle of mindless, emotional eating, reducing overeating and its associated guilt and anxiety.
    - By encouraging a non-judgmental awareness of eating habits, it supports a more positive relationship with food, reducing food-related anxiety.
    - Mindful eating can promote a sense of control and intentionality over one's dietary choices, which can alleviate anxiety related to perceived loss of control.

The Gut-Brain Connection:

- **Understanding the Gut-Brain Connection:** The gut-brain connection refers to the bi-directional communication between the gastrointestinal system (the gut) and the brain. This complex interplay involves neural, hormonal, and immune pathways.

- **The Role of the Gut Microbiota:** The gut is home to a vast ecosystem of microorganisms, collectively known as the gut microbiota. These microorganisms play a pivotal role in digestion, nutrient absorption, and the production of various bioactive compounds.

- **Impact on Anxiety**: Emerging research suggests that the gut-brain connection is intimately linked to mental health, including anxiety. Here's how:
    - Neurotransmitter Production: The gut microbiota influences the production of neurotransmitters like serotonin, which play a key role in mood regulation.
    - Inflammation: An unhealthy gut can lead to systemic inflammation, which is associated with mood disorders, including anxiety.
    - Communication Pathways: The gut and brain communicate through the vagus nerve and other signaling molecules, influencing emotional states.

- Diet and Gut Health: Diet significantly affects the composition of the gut microbiota. Consuming a diet rich in fiber, probiotics, and prebiotics (found in foods like yogurt, kefir, and certain fruits and vegetables) can promote a healthy gut microbiota, potentially reducing the risk of anxiety.

Nutritional Considerations:

Balanced Eating Defined: *Balanced eating involves consuming a wide variety of foods from different food groups in proportions that provide essential nutrients to maintain overall health.*

- **Components of Balanced Eating:**
    - Fruits and Vegetables: These are rich in vitamins, minerals, antioxidants, and fiber, which support physical and mental well-being.
    - Whole Grains: Whole grains like brown rice, oats, and quinoa provide complex carbohydrates for sustained energy and fiber for digestive health.
    - Proteins: Lean sources of protein such as poultry, fish, legumes, and tofu supply essential amino acids required for neurotransmitter synthesis.
    - Healthy Fats: Unsaturated fats from sources like avocados, nuts, and olive oil contribute to brain health.

- Hydration: Staying well-hydrated is vital for cognitive function and overall well-being.

- **Impact on Anxiety:** Nutritional considerations play a significant role in anxiety management:
    - Adequate intake of nutrients like B vitamins, magnesium, and omega-3 fatty acids supports the production of neurotransmitters involved in mood regulation.
    - Balanced eating can help stabilize blood sugar levels, preventing mood swings and reducing anxiety symptoms.
    - A healthy diet supports overall physical health, which has a direct influence on mental well-being.

Balanced eating and mindful eating are complementary approaches to nourishing both the body and mind. They contribute to physical health, support mood regulation, and can be valuable tools in the holistic management of anxiety. Additionally, recognizing the gut-brain connection underscores the importance of considering not only what we eat but also how it affects the intricate interplay between the gut and brain in relation
to anxiety.

Balanced Eating

Balanced Eating Defined: *Balanced eating, often referred to as a balanced diet or balanced nutrition, is an approach to food consumption that involves making mindful and intentional choices to provide the body with the necessary nutrients it needs for optimal physical and mental well-being.*

This approach emphasizes variety, moderation, and portion control in food selection, considering the following components:

Fruits and Vegetables:
- Rich in Nutrients: Fruits and vegetables are packed with essential vitamins, minerals, antioxidants, and dietary fiber.
- Mood Support: They contribute to overall health and provide nutrients such as vitamin C and folate, which are linked to mood regulation.

- Diversity: A variety of colorful fruits and vegetables ensures a broad spectrum of nutrients.

Whole Grains:
- Complex Carbohydrates: Whole grains like brown rice, oats, quinoa, and whole wheat provide complex carbohydrates that offer sustained energy.
- Fiber: They are rich in dietary fiber, which aids in digestion and helps maintain stable blood sugar levels.

Proteins:
- Lean Sources: Lean proteins such as poultry, fish, legumes, tofu, and lean cuts of meat supply essential amino acids required for neurotransmitter synthesis.
- Satiation: Proteins contribute to a feeling of fullness, preventing overeating.

Healthy Fats:
- Unsaturated Fats: Sources of healthy fats like avocados, nuts, seeds, and olive oil are essential for brain health.
- Omega-3 Fatty Acids: Fatty fish (e.g., salmon, mackerel) provide omega-3 fatty acids, which are associated with improved mood and reduced anxiety.

Hydration:
- Cognitive Function: Staying well-hydrated is vital for cognitive function and maintaining overall well-being.
- Balanced Electrolytes: Proper hydration helps balance electrolytes and supports the body's physiological processes.

Impact on Anxiety: Balanced eating plays a crucial role in anxiety management for several reasons:

- Nutrient Sufficiency: A balanced diet ensures that the body receives a broad spectrum of nutrients, including those essential for brain health and neurotransmitter production.
- Stable Blood Sugar: It helps stabilize blood sugar levels, preventing mood swings and reducing anxiety symptoms associated with blood sugar fluctuations.

- Physical Well-Being: Good physical health is closely linked to mental well-being. A diet rich in nutrients supports overall health, which in turn positively influences mental health.
- Satiety: Adequate protein and fiber intake contribute to feelings of fullness and prevent overeating, reducing the risk of anxiety-related emotional eating.

Balanced eating is not about strict diets or deprivation but rather about making informed choices that support overall health and well-being. When combined with mindful eating practices, it can contribute significantly to the holistic management of anxiety by providing the body and mind with the essential nutrients they need to thrive.

Section 2: Exercise and Physical Activity

Exercise isn't just beneficial for physical health; it's a powerful tool for managing anxiety and enhancing mental well-being. This section explores the relationship between physical activity and anxiety:

- **The Role of Exercise**: Understand how exercise releases endorphins, reduces stress hormones, and promotes a sense of well-being.
- **Types of Physical Activity**: Explore various forms of physical activity, from aerobic exercises like running and swimming to calming practices like yoga and tai chi.
- **Incorporating Exercise**: Learn practical strategies for incorporating regular physical activity into your routine, even if you have a busy schedule.
- **Social and Emotional Benefits**: Discover how exercise can improve self-esteem, reduce social anxiety, and foster a sense of accomplishment.

In this section, we will delve into the crucial role of exercise in managing anxiety and explore various aspects related to physical activity:

The Role of Exercise:

- **Physical and Mental Health Connection:** Exercise plays a multifaceted role in anxiety management. It's not just about physical fitness; it also has a profound impact on mental health.

Regular exercise can help reduce anxiety symptoms and enhance overall well-being.

- **Neurotransmitter Regulation:** Exercise triggers the release of endorphins, which are natural mood lifters. Additionally, it increases the availability of neurotransmitters like serotonin and norepinephrine, which are involved in mood regulation.

- **Stress Reduction:** Physical activity acts as a stress buffer, helping the body and mind better cope with stressors. It reduces the production of stress hormones like cortisol.

- **Enhanced Sleep:** Regular exercise can improve sleep quality, which is closely linked to anxiety. Adequate sleep helps regulate mood and reduce feelings of anxiety.

Types of Physical Activity:

- **Aerobic Exercise:** Activities like jogging, swimming, dancing, and cycling get the heart rate up and improve cardiovascular fitness. Aerobic exercise is particularly effective at releasing endorphins and reducing anxiety.

- **Strength Training:** Resistance training, using weights or resistance bands, helps build muscle strength and can boost self-esteem and body image, contributing to reduced anxiety.

- **Yoga and Mind-Body Practices:** Yoga combines physical postures, breathwork, and meditation. It promotes relaxation, reduces muscle tension, and fosters mindfulness, all of which are beneficial for anxiety management.

- **Outdoor Activities:** Spending time in nature, hiking, or simply going for a walk in a park can have a calming effect and reduce anxiety symptoms.

Incorporating Exercise:

- **Setting Realistic Goals:** It's essential to start with achievable goals and gradually increase the intensity and duration of exercise. Setting manageable targets helps maintain motivation.

- **Consistency:** Consistency is key to reaping the mental health benefits of exercise. Establishing a regular exercise routine ensures that the positive effects on anxiety are sustained.

- **Variety:** Mixing up exercise routines by trying different activities can prevent boredom and keep motivation high. Variety also challenges different muscle groups.

- **Social Support:** Exercising with friends or joining group fitness classes can provide social support, making exercise more enjoyable and fostering a sense of community.

Social and Emotional Benefits:

- **Stress Reduction**: Exercise helps reduce the physical and emotional effects of stress. It encourages the body to release tension and promotes relaxation.

- **Improved Self-Esteem:** Achieving fitness goals and experiencing physical improvements can boost self-esteem and self-confidence, reducing anxiety related to self-worth.

- **Enhanced Mood:** Regular exercise is associated with a more positive mood and a reduced risk of mood disorders. It can be an effective tool in managing symptoms of anxiety and depression.

- **Social Interaction:** Engaging in group activities or team sports provides opportunities for social interaction, reducing feelings of isolation and loneliness, which can contribute to anxiety.

Incorporating regular exercise into one's routine is a valuable strategy for managing anxiety. It not only has direct effects on neurotransmitters and stress hormones but also offers a range of social and emotional benefits that contribute to improved overall mental well-being.

Section 3: Sleep Hygiene

Quality sleep is fundamental to mental health and well-being. This section explores the importance of sleep hygiene practices for managing anxiety:

- **Understanding Sleep Hygiene**: Define sleep hygiene and its role in promoting restful and restorative sleep.
- **Sleep and Anxiety**: Explore the bidirectional relationship between anxiety and sleep, with practical strategies for breaking the cycle.
- **Creating a Sleep-Enhancing Environment**: Learn how to create a sleep-conducive environment and establish a bedtime routine that promotes better sleep.
- **Managing Sleep Disturbances**: Understand common sleep disturbances associated with anxiety, such as insomnia or nightmares, and strategies for addressing them.

By the end of this chapter, you'll have gained valuable insights into the impact of diet, exercise, and sleep on anxiety management. You'll also have a toolkit of practical techniques and strategies to help you make informed choices about nutrition, physical activity, and sleep hygiene, fostering holistic well-being and resilience.

In this section, we will explore the significance of sleep hygiene, the relationship between sleep and anxiety, strategies for creating a sleep-enhancing environment, and managing sleep disturbances:

Understanding Sleep Hygiene:

Definition: *Sleep hygiene refers to a set of practices and habits that promote healthy and restorative sleep. It involves creating a sleep-conducive environment and adopting bedtime routines that optimize sleep quality.*

- **Importance:** Good sleep hygiene is essential for overall well-being. It helps individuals fall asleep faster, stay asleep longer, and wake up feeling refreshed and alert.

- **Key Sleep Hygiene Practices:**
    - Consistent Sleep Schedule: Going to bed and waking up at the same time every day helps regulate the body's internal clock.

- Limiting Exposure to Screens: The blue light emitted by screens can interfere with the production of the sleep hormone melatonin. It's advisable to avoid screens before bedtime.
- Creating a Comfortable Sleep Environment: A comfortable mattress, suitable room temperature, and minimal noise and light contribute to better sleep.
- Avoiding Stimulants: Caffeine, nicotine, and alcohol can disrupt sleep patterns. It's best to avoid these substances close to bedtime.

Sleep and Anxiety:

- **Bidirectional Relationship:** Anxiety and sleep have a complex, bidirectional relationship. Anxiety can lead to sleep disturbances, including difficulty falling asleep, waking up during the night, or experiencing restless sleep.

- **Sleep Deprivation and Anxiety:** Chronic sleep deprivation can exacerbate anxiety symptoms and increase vulnerability to stress. It affects mood regulation and cognitive function.

- **Anxiety Dreams:** Anxiety can manifest in the form of vivid and distressing dreams, leading to sleep disruptions and further exacerbating anxiety.

Creating a Sleep-Enhancing Environment:

- **Optimal Sleep Environment:** A sleep-friendly environment promotes better sleep quality. Consider the following factors:
  - Darkness: A dark room helps trigger the production of melatonin, the sleep hormone.
  - Comfort: A comfortable mattress and pillows are essential for physical relaxation.
  - Noise Control: Reducing noise, using earplugs or white noise machines, can improve sleep quality.
  - Temperature: A cooler room temperature is generally conducive to sleep.

- **Bedtime Routine:** Establishing a calming bedtime routine signals to the body that it's time to wind down. This can include activities like reading, gentle stretching, or meditation.

Managing Sleep Disturbances:

- **Common Sleep Disturbances:** Sleep disturbances can take various forms, including insomnia (difficulty falling or staying asleep), sleep apnea, and restless leg syndrome, among others.

- **Seeking Professional Help:** Persistent or severe sleep disturbances should be evaluated by a healthcare professional. They can identify underlying causes and recommend appropriate treatments or therapies.

- **Cognitive-Behavioral Therapy for Insomnia (CBT-I):** CBT-I is a proven therapeutic approach for addressing insomnia. It helps individuals identify and modify the thoughts and behaviors that contribute to sleep difficulties.

- **Medication:** In some cases, healthcare providers may prescribe medications to manage sleep disturbances. These should be used under professional guidance and for a limited duration.

Addressing sleep hygiene and prioritizing healthy sleep habits are essential components of anxiety management. Adequate, restorative sleep not only reduces anxiety symptoms but also enhances overall physical and mental well-being. By creating a sleep-enhancing environment and managing sleep disturbances, individuals can significantly improve their sleep quality and, in turn, their anxiety levels.

Chapter 10: Building Resilience

Resilience is a critical life skill that empowers teenagers to bounce back from adversity and thrive in the face of challenges. This chapter explores the significance of resilience, strategies for developing resilience in teens, and how to overcome setbacks and challenges on the path to personal growth and well-being.

Section 1: The Importance of Resilience

Resilience is not just a trait; it's a dynamic process that can be nurtured and strengthened over time. This section delves into the profound importance of resilience:

- **Defining Resilience**: Understand what resilience means and how it differs from mere survival, highlighting its capacity to lead to growth and transformation.
- **The Resilience Advantage**: Explore the advantages of resilience, such as increased emotional well-being, adaptability, and the ability to cope with stress.
- **Resilience in Teenagers**: Recognize why resilience is particularly crucial during the teenage years, a period marked by significant transitions and challenges.
- **The Role of Support Systems**: Learn how supportive relationships, including family, friends, and mentors, play a crucial role in building and sustaining resilience.

In this section, we will explore the concept of resilience, its advantages, its relevance for teenagers, and the pivotal role of support systems in fostering resilience:

Defining Resilience:

Definition: *Resilience refers to the ability to adapt, bounce back, and maintain psychological well-being in the face of adversity, stress, or challenging life events. It's the capacity to endure difficulties, recover from setbacks, and grow stronger through adversity.*

- **Resilience Traits:** Resilient individuals often possess traits such as adaptability, optimism, problem-solving skills, emotional regulation, and a sense of purpose. These traits enable them to navigate life's ups and downs effectively.

- **Dynamic Process:** Resilience is not a fixed trait but a dynamic process. It can be cultivated and strengthened over time through experiences and intentional efforts.

The Resilience Advantage:

- **Enhanced Coping:** Resilience equips individuals with effective coping strategies, allowing them to manage stress and anxiety more efficiently.

- **Positive Outlook:** Resilient individuals tend to maintain a more positive outlook on life, even in challenging circumstances. This optimistic perspective can buffer against the development of anxiety and depression.

- **Growth and Learning:** Through adversity, resilient individuals often experience personal growth and learning. They develop valuable life skills and a deeper understanding of themselves.

Resilience in Teenagers:

- **Unique Challenges**: Teenagers face a unique set of challenges and stressors, including academic pressures, peer relationships, identity development, and the transition to adulthood. These challenges can contribute to anxiety and stress.

- **Building Resilience in Teens:** Fostering resilience in teenagers is crucial for their emotional well-being. Teaching them to cope effectively with challenges and setbacks can prepare them for a more resilient adulthood.

- **Developmental Opportunities**: Adolescence is a critical period for the development of resilience. It's a time when teens can learn and practice important life skills related to emotional regulation, problem-solving, and social connections.

The Role of Support Systems:

- **Family Support:** A strong and supportive family environment is a key factor in building resilience in teenagers. Families that provide emotional support, open communication, and a sense of security contribute significantly to a teen's resilience.

- **School and Community:** Schools and communities also play vital roles in nurturing resilience. Supportive teachers, mentors, and extracurricular activities can provide teens with opportunities to develop skills and build social connections.

- **Peer Relationships:** Peer relationships are central to a teenager's life. Positive friendships can be a source of support, offering empathy, companionship, and opportunities for shared problem-solving.

- **Mental Health Services:** Access to mental health services and professionals is essential for teens facing significant anxiety or trauma. Seeking help when needed is a crucial aspect of building resilience.

Understanding resilience and its significance in the context of teenage anxiety is essential for both teens and their support systems. It empowers individuals to develop the skills and mindset needed to face challenges with confidence, reduce anxiety, and thrive in the face of adversity. Building resilience is a lifelong journey, and starting during adolescence provides a strong foundation for future well-being.

Section 2: Developing Resilience in Teens

Resilience is a skill that can be cultivated and nurtured, even in the face of anxiety and adversity. This section provides strategies for developing resilience in teenagers:

- **Fostering a Growth Mindset**: Understand the concept of a growth mindset, which encourages a positive attitude toward challenges and learning from failures.
- **Emotional Regulation**: Explore techniques for managing emotions, such as mindfulness and emotional intelligence, to build emotional resilience.
- **Problem-Solving Skills**: Learn problem-solving strategies that empower teens to tackle challenges and setbacks with confidence.
- **Building Self-Efficacy**: Discover the importance of self-efficacy—the belief in one's ability to overcome difficulties—and how to nurture it in teenagers.

Fostering a Growth Mindset:

Definition: *Fostering a growth mindset means encouraging the belief that abilities and intelligence can be developed through effort, learning, and perseverance. It contrasts with a fixed mindset, which assumes that abilities are innate and unchangeable.*

- **Resilience Benefits:** Cultivating a growth mindset is foundational for resilience. When teenagers embrace the idea that challenges are opportunities for growth and view setbacks as part of the learning process, they are more likely to approach difficulties with determination and less likely to succumb to anxiety related to failure or mistakes.

- **Encouraging Effort:** Parents, teachers, and mentors can promote a growth mindset by praising effort, persistence, and the use of effective strategies rather than just innate talent. Reinforcing the idea that learning involves setbacks and mistakes helps teenagers develop resilience in the face of challenges.

Emotional Regulation:

Definition: *Emotional regulation refers to the ability to recognize, understand, and manage one's own emotions effectively. It involves strategies for coping with emotional experiences in a healthy and* *adaptive manner.*

- **Resilience Benefits:** Emotional regulation is a crucial component of resilience. When teenagers can identify their emotions, understand what triggers them, and respond to those emotions in constructive ways, they are better equipped to navigate stress and anxiety. Effective emotional regulation reduces the emotional toll of challenging situations.

- **Techniques:** Adolescents can learn various techniques for emotional regulation, including mindfulness practices, deep breathing exercises, journaling, and seeking support from trusted individuals. These strategies empower them to manage anxiety-provoking emotions more effectively.

    - **Mindfulness Meditation:** Mindfulness involves paying non-judgmental attention to the present moment. Regular mindfulness meditation can help teenagers become more aware of their emotions and manage them effectively. Apps and online resources offer guided mindfulness sessions tailored to teens.

    - **Deep Breathing:** Deep breathing exercises, such as diaphragmatic breathing, can help teenagers calm their nervous system and reduce anxiety. One technique is the 4-7-8 breathing method: inhale for 4 seconds, hold for 7 seconds, and exhale for 8 seconds.

    - **Journaling:** Encourage teenagers to keep a journal where they can write about their emotions, thoughts, and experiences. Journaling provides a healthy outlet for processing emotions and gaining insight into their triggers.

    - **Progressive Muscle Relaxation:** This technique involves systematically tensing and then relaxing different muscle groups. It can help alleviate physical tension that often accompanies emotional stress.

    - **Self-Compassion:** Teach teenagers to practice self-compassion by treating themselves with the same kindness and understanding they would offer a friend. Self-compassion can counter negative self-talk and reduce self-criticism.

Problem-Solving Skills:

Definition: *Problem-solving skills involve the ability to identify issues, generate potential solutions, evaluate those solutions, and choose the most appropriate course of action. Effective problem-solving contributes to a sense of control and agency.*

- **Resilience Benefits:** Problem-solving skills empower teenagers to address challenges and setbacks proactively. When they can break down problems into manageable steps, consider multiple solutions, and take action, they feel more confident in their ability to overcome adversity. This confidence reduces anxiety related to uncertainty.

- **Application:** Adolescents can develop problem-solving skills through practice. Encouraging them to tackle real-life issues, set goals, and work through obstacles provides valuable experiences for building resilience.

- **Problem-Solving Techniques:**
    - Identify the Problem: The first step in problem-solving is to clearly define the problem. Encourage teenagers to articulate what is bothering them and be as specific as possible.

    - Generate Potential Solutions: Brainstorming is a creative way to generate possible solutions to the problem. Encourage teens to think of multiple solutions, even if some seem far-fetched.

    - Evaluate and Choose a Solution: Once potential solutions are identified, help teenagers evaluate each one. Discuss the pros and cons of each option and consider the potential consequences. Together, choose the most appropriate solution.

    - Create an Action Plan: After selecting a solution, guide teenagers in creating a step-by-step action plan. Break down the plan into manageable tasks with clear deadlines.

    - Implement the Solution: Encourage teens to put their plan into action. This may involve seeking support from others, gathering necessary resources, or making specific changes in their behavior.

- ○ Review and Adjust: After implementing the solution, it's essential to assess its effectiveness. Did it solve the problem, or are adjustments needed? If necessary, return to the problem-solving process and try a different approach.

- ○ Seek Support: Teach teenagers that it's okay to seek support from trusted adults or peers when facing complex problems. Sometimes, an external perspective can provide valuable insights.

These emotional regulation techniques and problem-solving strategies empower teenagers to manage their emotions and navigate challenges more effectively. Encourage them to practice these techniques regularly and provide guidance and support as needed.

Building Self-Efficacy:

Definition: *Self-efficacy refers to an individual's belief in their ability to achieve specific goals and tasks. It's closely related to self-confidence and plays a significant role in motivation and resilience.*

- **Resilience Benefits:** When teenagers have a strong sense of self-efficacy, they approach challenges with confidence and determination. They believe they have the capability to overcome obstacles, which reduces anxiety related to self-doubt and uncertainty.

- **Developing Self-Efficacy:** Parents, teachers, and mentors can help teenagers build self-efficacy by providing opportunities for success, offering constructive feedback, and encouraging them to take on progressively more challenging tasks. Recognizing and celebrating their achievements reinforces their belief in their abilities.

Fostering a growth mindset, teaching emotional regulation, developing problem-solving skills, and building self-efficacy are essential strategies for equipping teenagers with the resilience they need to navigate life's challenges with confidence and reduce anxiety-related stress.

Section 3: Overcoming Setbacks and Challenges

Resilience is most evident when facing setbacks and challenges head-on. This section provides guidance on navigating adversity and using it as an opportunity for growth:

- **Navigating Setbacks**: Learn how to approach setbacks and disappointments as opportunities for learning and growth rather than as insurmountable obstacles.
- **Coping Strategies**: Explore practical coping strategies, such as reframing negative thoughts, seeking support, and using mindfulness, to overcome adversity.
- **Resilience and Anxiety**: Understand the relationship between resilience and anxiety, and how building resilience can help teenagers better manage anxiety.
- **Cultivating Resilience Over Time**: Recognize that resilience is an ongoing process that evolves with time and experience, and that setbacks are an inherent part of growth.

By the end of this chapter, you'll have a comprehensive understanding of the importance of resilience, practical strategies for nurturing resilience in teenagers, and the tools to help teens overcome setbacks and challenges, ultimately empowering them to thrive in the face of adversity.

Navigating Setbacks:

Definition: *Navigating setbacks refers to the process of handling and recovering from disappointments, failures, or obstacles in life. Setbacks are a normal part of life, and how teenagers respond to them can significantly impact their resilience.*

- **Resilience Building:** Setbacks provide opportunities for teenagers to develop resilience. When they encounter setbacks, they can learn valuable lessons about perseverance, problem-solving, and adaptability. Encourage teenagers to view setbacks as temporary challenges that can be overcome.

- **Managing Emotions:** Setbacks often evoke strong emotions such as frustration, disappointment, or sadness. Teach teenagers healthy ways to manage these emotions, such as talking to a trusted friend or family member, journaling, or engaging in relaxation techniques.

Coping Strategies:

Definition: *Coping strategies are techniques and behaviors that individuals use to manage stress, anxiety, and difficult emotions. Effective coping strategies can significantly enhance a teenager's ability to bounce back from adversity.*

- **Types of Coping Strategies:** Coping strategies can be categorized into two main types: problem-focused and emotion-focused. Problem-focused coping involves taking direct action to address the source of stress or problem. Emotion-focused coping focuses on managing the emotional response to stress.

- **Problem-Focused Coping:** Encourage teenagers to identify specific actions they can take to address a problem or stressor. Problem-solving, time management, and seeking support are examples of problem-focused coping strategies.

- **Emotion-Focused Coping:** Sometimes, it's essential to manage the emotional response to stress. Techniques like mindfulness, relaxation exercises, and seeking emotional support from friends or family are examples of emotion-focused coping.

Resilience and Anxiety:

- **Relationship Between Resilience and Anxiety**: Resilience and anxiety are closely connected. Higher levels of resilience can reduce the risk of developing anxiety disorders and help individuals manage anxiety symptoms more effectively.

- **Resilience as a Protective Factor:** Resilience acts as a protective factor against anxiety. When teenagers possess strong resilience skills, they are better equipped to cope with stressors, adapt to changes, and bounce back from challenging situations without succumbing to overwhelming anxiety.

- **Cultivating Resilience to Manage Anxiety:** Anxiety management often involves developing resilience skills. Through strategies like problem-solving, emotional regulation, and seeking support, teenagers can build resilience that helps them cope with anxiety triggers and reduce anxiety symptoms.

Cultivating Resilience Over Time:

- **Developmental Process:** Cultivating resilience is a developmental process that unfolds over time. It's not something that happens overnight but rather through a series of experiences, challenges, and personal growth.

- **Lifelong Skill:** Resilience is a lifelong skill that teenagers can continue to develop into adulthood. Encourage them to view resilience as an ongoing journey rather than a destination.

- **Support and Guidance:** As teenagers cultivate resilience, they benefit from the support and guidance of parents, teachers, mentors, and mental health professionals. These individuals can provide valuable insights, encouragement, and resources to facilitate resilience building.

- **Learning from Experience:** Part of cultivating resilience involves learning from both successes and failures. Encourage teenagers to reflect on their experiences, identify strengths, and consider how they can apply their resilience skills in future challenges.

Helping teenagers navigate setbacks, develop effective coping strategies, understand the connection between resilience and anxiety, and appreciate that resilience is a lifelong skill that empowers them to approach life's ups and downs with greater confidence and well-being.

Chapter 11: Seeking Professional Help

Therapy can be a crucial resource for teenagers struggling with anxiety. This chapter explores the signs that indicate it may be time to consider therapy, the role of school counselors, and how to find the right therapist to provide the support needed.

Section 1: When to Consider Therapy

Recognizing when therapy may be beneficial is a vital step in addressing anxiety. In this section, we explore the signs and situations that indicate it may be time to seek professional help:

- **Persistent Anxiety Symptoms**: Learn how to distinguish between normal anxiety and persistent, debilitating anxiety that may require therapeutic intervention.
- **Interference with Daily Life**: Understand how anxiety can interfere with daily activities, school, relationships, and overall well-being, serving as a red flag for therapy.
- **Physical Symptoms**: Explore the physical manifestations of anxiety, such as panic attacks, sleep disturbances, and psychosomatic symptoms, which may warrant therapeutic support.
- **Self-Harm or Suicidal Thoughts**: Recognize the urgency of seeking therapy when teenagers engage in self-harm or experience suicidal thoughts or behaviors.

Persistent Anxiety Symptoms:

Definition: Persistent anxiety symptoms refer to feelings of unease, fear, or worry that endure over an extended period. While it's normal to experience occasional anxiety, persistent symptoms can be a sign of an anxiety disorder.

- Common Symptoms: Anxiety symptoms can manifest in various ways, including excessive worry, restlessness, irritability, muscle tension, and difficulty concentrating. In teenagers, these symptoms may interfere with daily activities, academic performance, and relationships.

- Importance of Identification: Identifying and addressing persistent anxiety symptoms early is crucial. These symptoms can have a profound impact on a teenager's well-being, and early intervention can prevent the worsening of anxiety disorders.

Interference with Daily Life:

Definition: Anxiety that interferes with daily life refers to the extent to which anxiety symptoms disrupt a teenager's ability to engage in typical activities and responsibilities.

- Academic Performance: Anxiety can hinder a teenager's academic performance by causing difficulty concentrating, procrastination, and test anxiety. It may lead to lower grades and missed opportunities.

- Social and Family Life: Anxiety can affect a teenager's relationships with peers and family members. Social anxiety, for example, can lead to avoidance of social situations, making it challenging to maintain friendships and family connections.

- Physical Health: Persistent anxiety can also impact physical health by contributing to sleep disturbances, digestive issues, and tension-related ailments like headaches or muscle pain.

- Long-Term Consequences: When anxiety significantly interferes with daily life, it can lead to long-term consequences such as lowered self-esteem, decreased quality of life, and a higher risk of developing comorbid mental health conditions.

Physical Symptoms:

- **Physical Manifestations:** Anxiety often presents with physical symptoms, even in the absence of a specific stressor. These symptoms can include rapid heartbeat, shortness of breath, trembling, sweating, dizziness, and nausea.

- **Fight-or-Flight Response:** These physical symptoms are part of the body's natural "fight-or-flight" response to stress. While this response is adaptive in the short term, chronic anxiety can keep these physical symptoms persistently activated, contributing to discomfort and distress.

- **Health Impact:** Persistent physical symptoms of anxiety can negatively impact a teenager's health. They may lead to chronic stress-related conditions and exacerbate preexisting health issues.

- **Misinterpretation:** Teenagers experiencing physical symptoms of anxiety may misinterpret them as signs of a severe medical condition, which can further exacerbate anxiety. Education about the physical manifestations of anxiety is essential for reducing unnecessary distress.

Self-Harm or Suicidal Thoughts:

- **Emergent Concerns:** When anxiety becomes severe and persistent, it can lead to more concerning behaviors, such as self-harm or suicidal thoughts. These behaviors are indicative of significant emotional distress and should be taken seriously.

- **Risk Factors**: Teenagers with persistent anxiety may be at a higher risk of self-harm or suicidal thoughts, particularly if they feel trapped, hopeless, or overwhelmed by their symptoms.

- **Immediate Intervention:** Any indication of self-harm or suicidal thoughts requires immediate intervention. Parents, caregivers, educators, and mental health professionals should provide support, ensure the teenager's safety, and connect them with appropriate mental health resources.

- **Importance of Open Communication**: Creating an environment where teenagers feel safe discussing their emotions and struggles is crucial for early intervention. Encourage open communication and let them know that seeking help is a sign of strength.

Recognizing the signs of persistent anxiety symptoms, understanding how they interfere with daily life, acknowledging the physical manifestations, and being vigilant about self-harm or suicidal thoughts are essential steps in addressing anxiety-related challenges in teenagers and ensuring their well-being. Early intervention and access to mental health support can make a significant difference in their recovery and long-term mental health.

Section 2: The Role of School Counselors

School counselors play a vital role in supporting teenagers' mental health and well-being. This section delves into the responsibilities of school counselors and how they can assist students dealing with anxiety:

- **Counseling Services in Schools**: Understand the types of counseling services available in schools, ranging from academic support to emotional counseling.
- **Identifying Students in Need**: Learn how school counselors identify students who may benefit from counseling and the steps they take to provide support.
- **Collaboration with Parents and Teachers**: Explore how school counselors collaborate with parents, teachers, and other professionals to create a supportive network for students.
- **Confidentiality and Trust**: Understand the importance of confidentiality in the counseling relationship and how school counselors build trust with students.

Counseling Services in Schools:

Definition: *Counseling services in schools refer to the provision of mental health support and counseling within an educational setting. School counselors or mental health professionals play a crucial role in helping students navigate emotional, social, and academic challenges.*

- **Services Offered:** School-based counseling services encompass a range of interventions, including individual counseling, group counseling, crisis intervention, and psychoeducation. These services are designed to address students' emotional well-being, mental health concerns, and personal development.

- **Accessibility**: Having counseling services within the school environment enhances accessibility for students. It eliminates barriers related to transportation, stigma, and scheduling conflicts, making it easier for students to seek help when needed.

- **Preventive and Supportive:** School counselors not only address existing mental health issues but also work preventively by promoting mental health awareness, providing coping strategies, and helping students develop essential life skills.

Identifying Students in Need:

- **Early Identification:** Identifying students in need of counseling services is a critical aspect of school-based mental health support. Early identification allows for timely intervention, which can prevent the escalation of mental health issues.

- **Multiple Sources of Referral:** School counselors often receive referrals from multiple sources, including teachers, parents, self-referrals by students, or observations of concerning behaviors. Collaboration among these stakeholders is key to identifying students in need.

- **Screening Programs:** Some schools implement screening programs to assess students' emotional well-being and identify potential mental health concerns. These screenings can be especially valuable for early intervention.

- **Cultural Sensitivity:** It's essential to approach the identification process with cultural sensitivity, recognizing that different cultures may express and perceive mental health concerns differently. Schools should aim to provide inclusive and culturally competent services.

Collaboration with Parents and Teachers:

- **Team Approach:** Effective school-based counseling involves collaboration among school counselors, parents, and teachers. These stakeholders form a team that works together to support the well-being of the student.

- **Communication:** Regular and open communication is crucial. School counselors should keep parents and teachers informed about a student's progress, concerns, and any recommended interventions.

- **Parent Involvement:** Parents play a vital role in their child's mental health. School counselors can provide parents with resources, information, and strategies for supporting their child's emotional well-being at home.

- **Teacher Support:** Teachers can provide valuable insights into a student's behavior and academic performance. School counselors can collaborate with teachers to develop strategies for addressing specific challenges a student may be facing.

Confidentiality and Trust:

- **Confidentiality:** Maintaining confidentiality is a fundamental principle of counseling. Students need to trust that what they discuss with a counselor will remain private, except in situations where there is a risk of harm to themselves or others.

- **Building Trust:** School counselors work diligently to build trust with students. Trust is essential for effective counseling relationships, as students are more likely to open up and seek support when they feel safe and heard.

- **Informed Consent:** School counselors typically inform students about the limits of confidentiality during the initial sessions. This helps students understand when information may need to be shared with other professionals or caregivers.

- **Safety Concerns:** While confidentiality is crucial, counselors prioritize the safety and well-being of students. If there are concerns about a student's safety, such as thoughts of self-harm or harm to others, counselors may need to breach confidentiality to ensure the student receives appropriate help.

School-based counseling services, when implemented effectively, provide valuable support to students by addressing their mental health needs, promoting well-being, and fostering a collaborative approach involving parents and teachers. Ensuring confidentiality and trust within these services is essential for creating a safe and supportive environment for students to seek help and thrive academically and emotionally.

Section 3: Finding the Right Therapist

Finding the right therapist is essential for effective anxiety management. This section offers guidance on the process of selecting a therapist who can best meet the needs of a teenager:

- **Types of Therapists**: Explore various types of mental health professionals, such as psychologists, counselors, social workers, and psychiatrists, and their respective specialties.
- **Therapeutic Approaches**: Understand different therapeutic approaches, such as Cognitive-Behavioral Therapy (CBT), Dialectical Behavior Therapy (DBT), and talk therapy, and how to choose the most suitable one.
- **Finding a Therapist**: Discover strategies for finding a therapist, including referrals from school counselors, healthcare providers, online directories, and recommendations from trusted sources.
- **Evaluating Compatibility**: Learn how to assess the compatibility between a teenager and a therapist, ensuring a strong therapeutic alliance.

By the end of this chapter, you'll have a clear understanding of when to consider therapy for anxiety, the valuable role of school counselors in the process, and practical guidance for finding the right therapist to provide the support and guidance needed to address anxiety effectively.

Types of Therapists:

- **Licensed Clinical Psychologists:** Clinical psychologists have doctoral degrees in psychology and are trained to diagnose and treat a wide range of mental health issues. They often use talk therapy techniques and evidence-based interventions.

- **Licensed Clinical Social Workers (LCSWs):** LCSWs have a master's degree in social work and are licensed to provide therapy. They specialize in helping individuals and families cope with various social and emotional challenges.

- **Licensed Professional Counselors (LPCs):** LPCs have master's degrees in counseling and are trained to provide therapy for various mental health concerns. They often use a variety of counseling techniques tailored to the individual's needs.

- **Psychiatrists:** Psychiatrists are medical doctors who can prescribe medication and provide therapy. They are often sought for more severe mental health conditions or when medication is considered necessary.

- **Licensed Marriage and Family Therapists (LMFTs):** LMFTs specialize in therapy for couples and families. They address relationship and family dynamics and can be valuable for adolescents experiencing family-related stress.

- **School Counselors:** Many schools have trained counselors who provide support to students within the educational setting. They can offer guidance and referrals for more specialized therapy if needed.

Therapeutic Approaches:

- **Cognitive-Behavioral Therapy (CBT):** CBT focuses on identifying and changing negative thought patterns and behaviors. It's effective for a wide range of mental health concerns, including anxiety and depression.

- **Dialectical Behavior Therapy (DBT):** DBT combines cognitive-behavioral techniques with mindfulness strategies. It's particularly helpful for adolescents struggling with emotional regulation.

- **Mindfulness-Based Therapy**: These approaches, such as Mindfulness-Based Stress Reduction (MBSR), teach mindfulness and meditation techniques to help adolescents manage stress, anxiety, and emotional reactivity.

- **Family Therapy**: Family therapy involves working with the entire family to address relational issues and improve communication. It can be beneficial when family dynamics contribute to the adolescent's challenges.

- **Play Therapy:** Play therapy is used with younger adolescents and involves using play and creative techniques to help them express themselves and work through emotional difficulties.

- **Humanistic and Person-Centered Therapy:** These approaches focus on the individual's self-acceptance and self-actualization. They emphasize empathy and understanding.

Finding a Therapist:

- **Recommendations**: Seek recommendations from trusted sources, such as your primary care physician, school counselor, or friends and family who have experience with therapy.

- **Online Directories:** Utilize online directories and databases provided by mental health organizations to find therapists in your area. Many directories include detailed profiles and specialties.

- **Health Insurance:** Check with your health insurance provider to see which therapists are covered by your plan. This can help narrow down your options.

- **Teletherapy**: Consider teletherapy options, which offer the flexibility of accessing therapy from the comfort of your home. This can be especially convenient for adolescents.

Evaluating Compatibility:

- **Initial Consultation**: Many therapists offer initial consultations, either in person or over the phone. This is an opportunity to discuss your concerns and assess whether you feel comfortable and heard.

- **Therapist's Style:** Different therapists have different therapeutic styles and personalities. It's important to find a therapist whose approach aligns with your preferences and needs.

- **Experience and Specialization**: Consider the therapist's experience and specialization. Some therapists specialize in working with adolescents and specific issues like anxiety or trauma.

- **Trust and Rapport:** Building a trusting and positive therapeutic relationship is essential. You should feel safe, respected, and understood by your therapist.

- **Communication:** Effective communication is key. Ensure that you and your therapist can communicate openly and honestly during sessions.

Finding the right therapist for an adolescent involves careful consideration of the therapist's qualifications, therapeutic approach, and compatibility with the adolescent's needs and preferences. It's important to take the time to find a therapist who can provide the support and guidance necessary for the adolescent's mental health and well-being.

Chapter 12: Support Systems for Teens

Support from family, peers, and the community is invaluable in managing teen anxiety. This chapter explores the importance of family support, building a strong peer network, and accessing community resources to create a robust safety net for teenagers dealing with anxiety.

Section 1: The Importance of Family Support

Family is often the first line of support for teenagers. This section emphasizes the role of family in managing anxiety:

- **Understanding Family Dynamics**: Explore how family dynamics can either exacerbate or alleviate anxiety in teenagers, and the impact of parental modeling of coping strategies.
- **Open Communication**: Learn the significance of open and empathetic communication within the family, including discussing anxiety and feelings without judgment.
- **Setting Realistic Expectations**: Understand how setting achievable expectations and goals can reduce stress and anxiety within the family unit.
- **Seeking Professional Help Together**: Discover the benefits of involving the family in therapy or counseling sessions to address anxiety as a collective challenge.

Understanding Family Dynamics:

- **Definition:** Family dynamics refer to the patterns of interaction, roles, and relationships within a family. Understanding these dynamics is crucial when addressing anxiety in adolescents because family dynamics can both influence and be influenced by the adolescent's anxiety.

- **Impact on Anxiety:** Family dynamics can contribute to or alleviate an adolescent's anxiety. For example, overprotective parenting, excessive criticism, or unresolved family conflicts can increase stress and anxiety. On the other hand, a supportive, communicative, and understanding family environment can be a protective factor.

- **Family Systems Theory:** Family therapists often use the family systems theory to explore how changes in one family member's behavior or emotions can ripple through the entire family system. Addressing anxiety in one family member may necessitate changes in how the family as a whole functions.

- **Family Therapy:** In cases where family dynamics are a significant contributor to an adolescent's anxiety, family therapy can be beneficial. Family therapists help identify unhealthy patterns and work with the family to develop more effective and supportive ways of relating to each other.

Open Communication:

Definition: *Open communication within a family means that family members feel comfortable discussing their thoughts, feelings, and concerns with each other. It fosters an environment where everyone's perspectives are valued.*

- **Benefits for Anxiety:** Open communication is a powerful tool for managing anxiety in adolescents. It allows them to express their worries and fears and receive support and understanding from family members. Knowing they can talk openly reduces the sense of isolation and loneliness that often accompanies anxiety.

- **Active Listening:** Active listening is a crucial component of open communication. Family members should listen without judgment, offer empathy, and validate the adolescent's feelings.

- **Problem-Solving:** Open communication facilitates problem-solving. When family members collaborate to address challenges, it can reduce anxiety triggers and promote a sense of control.

Setting Realistic Expectations:

Definition: *Setting realistic expectations involves establishing attainable goals and standards for the adolescent. Unrealistic expectations can create undue* *pressure and stress.*

- **Impact on Anxiety:** Adolescents may experience anxiety when they feel pressured to meet high academic, social, or behavioral standards. Setting realistic expectations means recognizing the adolescent's strengths and limitations and adjusting expectations accordingly.

- **Healthy Achievement:** Encourage a balanced approach to achievement that values effort, personal growth, and well-being. Emphasize that setbacks and mistakes are a natural part of learning and development.

- **Individualized Goals:** Work with the adolescent to set individualized goals that are meaningful to them. This helps them develop a sense of autonomy and motivation to work towards those goals.

Seeking Professional Help Together:

Definition: Seeking professional help together as a family involves involving a mental health professional to guide and support the family in addressing the adolescent's anxiety.

- **Benefits:** Involving a mental health professional can be highly beneficial when anxiety within the family is complex or longstanding. The therapist can provide insights, strategies, and a neutral perspective that can lead to positive changes.

- **Family Education:** Family therapy sessions often include education about anxiety disorders and their treatment. This knowledge can empower family members to better understand the adolescent's experiences and how to support them.

- **Skill Building:** Family therapy can teach the family communication and coping skills that enhance their ability to address anxiety effectively. These 10 skills can be applied to various challenges within the family.

    1. Active Listening Skills:
        a. Reflective Listening: Family members can practice reflective listening, where they paraphrase what the adolescent is saying to ensure they understand correctly. This helps the adolescent feel heard and validated.

     b.   Empathetic Responses: Encourage family members to respond empathetically to the adolescent's feelings. For example, saying, "I can see why that situation made you anxious" demonstrates empathy.

2. Effective Communication:
   a. Use "I" Statements: Teach family members to use "I" statements to express their own feelings and needs without blaming or accusing. For example, "I feel concerned when you don't communicate about your plans" is more constructive than "You never tell us anything."
   b. Conflict Resolution: Help family members develop conflict resolution skills. This includes active problem-solving and compromise. Family therapy can provide a structured environment for practicing these skills.

3. Emotional Regulation:
   a. Mindfulness Practices: Learn and practice mindfulness techniques as a family. Mindfulness exercises can help family members manage their own stress and emotions, which in turn can create a calmer family environment.
   b. Emotion Recognition: Work together to improve emotional awareness and recognition. This can help family members better understand and support each other's emotional needs.

4. Stress Management:
   a. Stress Reduction Strategies: Collaborate on identifying and implementing stress reduction strategies that work for each family member. These may include exercise, relaxation techniques, or hobbies.
   b. Time Management: Teach time management skills to help family members balance responsibilities, reduce procrastination, and create a less stressful daily routine.

5. Conflict Resolution:
   a. Active Problem-Solving: Practice active problem-solving as a family when conflicts arise. Encourage each family member to express their concerns and work together to find mutually agreeable solutions.

b.   Negotiation Skills: Teach negotiation skills to help family members reach compromises that meet everyone's needs. This can be especially valuable when conflicts involve different preferences or expectations.

6.   Boundaries and Self-Care:
   a.   Personal Boundaries: Discuss and establish healthy personal boundaries within the family. Everyone should have the right to their own space, time, and privacy.
   b.   Self-Care Practices: Promote self-care practices for each family member. Encourage activities that help individuals relax and recharge, such as reading, exercise, or hobbies.

7.   Supportive Responses:
   a.   Validation: Teach family members how to validate each other's feelings and experiences. Validation involves acknowledging the validity of the other person's perspective without judgment.
   b.   Encouragement: Encourage family members to provide positive reinforcement and encouragement for one another's efforts to manage anxiety and develop new skills.

8.   Relapse Prevention:
   a.   Identifying Triggers: Help the family identify common triggers of anxiety within the household. By recognizing these triggers, the family can work together to reduce their impact.
   b.   Developing Coping Strategies: Collaboratively develop a toolbox of coping strategies that family members can use when anxiety flares up. These strategies can include deep breathing exercises, grounding techniques, or relaxation routines.

9.   Education and Advocacy:
   a.   Mental Health Literacy: Educate family members about anxiety disorders and mental health in general. Understanding the nature of anxiety can reduce stigma and increase empathy.
   b.   Advocacy Skills: Encourage family members to advocate for the adolescent's mental health needs within the

school system or other relevant settings. This can involve communication with teachers, counselors, or healthcare providers.

- Building these skills as a family can not only support the adolescent with anxiety but also strengthen family bonds and create a more emotionally supportive environment. Family therapy sessions with a trained professional can provide a structured and safe space for practicing these skills and working collaboratively toward positive change.

- **Support and Validation:** Family therapy offers a safe space for family members to express their concerns and emotions. The therapist can facilitate understanding, empathy, and resolution of conflicts.

Addressing anxiety within the family context requires a multi-faceted approach that considers family dynamics, encourages open communication, sets realistic expectations, and, when necessary, seeks the guidance of a mental health professional. Building a supportive and understanding family environment can significantly contribute to an adolescent's ability to manage anxiety and promote their overall well-being.

Section 2: Building a Supportive Peer Network

Peers play a pivotal role in a teenager's life. This section explores how to build and leverage a supportive peer network:

- **Peer Empathy**: Understand how friends who demonstrate empathy and understanding can provide emotional support, reducing feelings of isolation.
- **Peer Pressure and Boundaries**: Learn strategies for navigating peer pressure, setting boundaries, and making choices that prioritize mental health.
- **Supportive Activities**: Explore the benefits of engaging in group activities or hobbies with peers that foster a sense of belonging and shared interests.
- **Seeking Help Together**: Understand the power of friends encouraging each other to seek help and providing emotional support during the therapeutic process.

Peer Empathy:

Definition: *Peer empathy refers to the ability of friends and peers to understand and share in the emotional experiences of adolescents dealing with anxiety. It involves being sensitive to their feelings, showing compassion, and offering support.*

- **Benefits:** Peer empathy can significantly benefit adolescents with anxiety. When peers are empathetic, it reduces feelings of isolation and stigma often associated with anxiety disorders. Knowing that their friends understand and care about their struggles can be emotionally reassuring.

- **Listening and Validation:** Being an empathetic peer involves active listening and validating the feelings of the adolescent. Friends can create a safe space where the adolescent feels comfortable expressing their worries and fears without judgment.

- **Encouragement:** Empathetic peers can provide encouragement and emotional support during difficult times. They can offer words of comfort and remind the adolescent that they are not alone in their journey.

Peer Pressure and Boundaries:

Definition: *Peer pressure is the influence that friends and peers can exert on one another's behavior and decision-making. Setting and maintaining healthy boundaries with peers is essential for adolescents dealing with anxiety.*

- **Awareness of Triggers:** Friends should be aware of potential anxiety triggers and be sensitive to situations that may cause distress for their anxious peer. This awareness can help them avoid putting undue pressure on the adolescent.

- **Respect for Boundaries:** Friends should respect the boundaries set by the anxious adolescent. For example, if the adolescent needs space or prefers not to engage in certain activities, their friends should honor those requests without judgment.

- **Supportive Decision-Making:** Encourage peers to support the anxious adolescent in making decisions that align with their well-being, even if those decisions differ from the group's choices. This might include opting out of certain social activities or taking breaks when needed.

Supportive Activities:

Definition: *Supportive activities involve engaging in hobbies, interests, or pastimes that provide emotional comfort and a sense of camaraderie. These activities can help reduce anxiety and create opportunities for bonding among peers.*

- **Examples:** Supportive activities can include going for walks together, participating in creative endeavors like art or music, or engaging in sports and exercise. These shared activities offer a break from stressors and provide opportunities for relaxation and fun.

- **Team Building:** Team-building activities, such as group games or projects, can help strengthen the bonds between peers and provide a sense of belonging. Adolescents with anxiety may benefit from these activities when they are conducted in a supportive and inclusive manner.

- **Positive Distractions**: Engaging in enjoyable activities can serve as positive distractions from anxious thoughts and worries. When friends provide opportunities for these distractions, it can be especially helpful for managing anxiety symptoms.

Seeking Help Together:

Definition: *Encouraging peers to seek help together means that friends can play a role in supporting the anxious adolescent in reaching out for professional assistance when needed.*

- **Destigmatization**: Friends can contribute to destigmatizing mental health issues by openly discussing the importance of seeking help and emphasizing that it's a sign of strength rather than weakness.

- **Accompanying to Appointments:** In some cases, friends may offer to accompany the anxious adolescent to therapy sessions or doctor's appointments, providing emotional support and reducing any feelings of apprehension about seeking help.

- **Encouragement:** Friends can provide ongoing encouragement and motivation for the adolescent to follow through with treatment recommendations and therapy. Their support can be instrumental in the treatment process.

Peer support is invaluable for adolescents dealing with anxiety. It creates a network of understanding and compassion that can significantly enhance the adolescent's well-being. When peers show empathy, respect boundaries, engage in supportive activities, and encourage seeking help when needed, they contribute to a nurturing and empathetic environment that can be transformative for the adolescent's mental health journey.

Section 3: Community Resources

Communities offer a wealth of resources to support teenagers with anxiety. This section explores the various resources available:

- **School-Based Resources**: Discover the range of mental health services available within schools, including counseling, support groups, and educational programs.
- **Local Organizations**: Learn about local nonprofit organizations, clubs, and initiatives focused on mental health and anxiety support for teenagers.
- **Online Communities**: Explore the benefits of online communities and forums where teenagers can connect with peers facing similar challenges.
- Community Events and Workshops: Understand the value of attending workshops, seminars, or events that focus on mental health and anxiety management.

By the end of this chapter, you'll have a comprehensive understanding of how family support, a supportive peer network, and community resources can form a robust safety net to help teenagers effectively manage anxiety. Additionally, you'll gain insights into how to access and leverage these sources of support to create a nurturing environment for teens.

School-Based Resources:

Definition: *School-based resources are the services and support systems available within the educational setting to assist students in managing their anxiety and mental health. These resources are often provided by school counselors, psychologists, and other professionals.*

- **Counseling Services:** Many schools have trained counselors who can offer individual or group counseling sessions to address anxiety and related concerns. These services can help students develop coping skills and strategies.

- **Peer Support Groups:** Some schools facilitate peer support groups where students with similar challenges, such as anxiety, can come together to share experiences and learn from one another. These groups can reduce feelings of isolation.

- **Academic Accommodations:** Schools may provide academic accommodations for students with anxiety, such as extended test-taking time or access to a quiet space for exams. These accommodations aim to reduce academic stress.

- **Education and Awareness:** School-based resources often include mental health education and awareness programs that help students and staff recognize the signs of anxiety and promote a stigma-free environment.

Local Organizations:

Definition: *Local organizations refer to non-profit or community-based groups and agencies that offer support and resources for adolescents dealing with anxiety and their families.*

- **Support Groups:** Local organizations may host support groups specifically designed for adolescents with anxiety or their parents. These groups provide a safe space for sharing experiences and advice.

- **Workshops and Training:** Some local organizations offer workshops and training sessions on topics related to anxiety management, stress reduction, and parenting skills. These can be valuable resources for adolescents and their families.

- **Access to Professionals:** Local organizations may partner with mental health professionals to provide low-cost or sliding-scale therapy services for adolescents who may not have easy access to such care.

- **Community Events:** These organizations often organize community events and awareness campaigns to reduce the stigma surrounding mental health issues and promote understanding.

Online Communities:

Definition: *Online communities are virtual spaces where adolescents dealing with anxiety can connect with others who share similar experiences. These communities can take the form of forums, social media groups, or dedicated websites.*

- **Peer Support:** Online communities offer a platform for peer support, allowing adolescents to share their stories, offer advice, and connect with individuals who understand what they're going through.

- **Information and Resources:** These communities often provide a wealth of information on anxiety management, coping strategies, and self-help resources. However, it's important to verify the credibility of the sources.

- **Anonymity and Accessibility:** Online communities provide a level of anonymity that can be appealing for adolescents who may be hesitant to share their struggles in person. They are accessible 24/7, which can be especially helpful during moments of distress.

- **Moderation and Safety:** It's essential to ensure that online communities are moderated and safe spaces, free from bullying or harmful content. Parents and caregivers should be aware of their adolescent's online interactions and guide them to reputable communities.

Community Events and Workshops:

Definition: *Community events and workshops are in-person or virtual gatherings organized by local institutions, mental health organizations, or community centers to provide information, support, and education on mental health and anxiety.*

- **Psychoeducation Workshops:** These workshops often focus on educating adolescents and their families about anxiety disorders, their symptoms, and effective coping strategies. They may also address related topics such as stress management and emotional regulation.

- **Community Support Groups:** Some community events bring together individuals facing similar challenges, such as anxiety or mood disorders, to share experiences and offer mutual support.

- **Awareness Campaigns:** Community events may include awareness campaigns that aim to reduce stigma surrounding mental health issues and encourage open conversations. These campaigns often involve panel discussions, guest speakers, or art exhibitions.

- **Resource Fairs:** Occasionally, community resource fairs are organized, where attendees can access information about local mental health services, support groups, and resources available to them.

Community resources and support play a vital role in providing adolescents with the tools, knowledge, and connections they need to effectively manage anxiety. Whether through school-based services, local organizations, online communities, or community events, these resources contribute to a more inclusive and supportive environment for adolescents and their families.

Chapter 13: Balancing School and Anxiety

Balancing academic success and managing anxiety can be challenging for teenagers. This chapter explores effective time management strategies, coping with test and homework anxiety, and seeking help and support at school to excel academically while maintaining mental well-being.

Section 1: Time Management Strategies

Effective time management is essential for reducing academic stress and anxiety. This section delves into time management strategies tailored for teenagers:

- **Prioritizing Tasks**: Learn how to identify and prioritize tasks, assignments, and activities to allocate time efficiently.
- **Creating a Schedule**: Understand the benefits of creating a daily or weekly schedule to organize academic and non-academic responsibilities.
- **Setting Realistic Goals**: Discover the importance of setting achievable goals and breaking them down into manageable steps to reduce overwhelm.
- **Avoiding Procrastination**: Explore techniques to overcome procrastination and stay focused on tasks, reducing last-minute stress.

Prioritizing Tasks:

Definition: *Prioritizing tasks involves identifying and ranking tasks or activities based on their importance and urgency. It helps adolescents focus their energy and time on what truly matters.*

- **Benefits for Anxiety:** Anxiety can often make adolescents feel overwhelmed by the sheer number of tasks they need to complete. Prioritization helps them break down their to-do list into manageable chunks, reducing feelings of being swamped.

- **Methods:** Adolescents can use various methods to prioritize tasks, such as the Eisenhower Matrix (quadrant method), where tasks are categorized as urgent/important, important/not urgent, urgent/not important, or neither. This method helps them allocate their time and effort effectively.

1. **The Eisenhower Matrix (Quadrant Method):**
   - **Overview:** The Eisenhower Matrix is a time management and prioritization tool that helps individuals categorize tasks based on their importance and urgency. It was popularized by former U.S. President Dwight D. Eisenhower and is often depicted as a 2x2 grid with four quadrants.

   - **Quadrants:**
     - Urgent and Important (Do First):
       - Definition: Tasks in this quadrant are both urgent and important. They require immediate attention and should be completed as a top priority.
       - Examples: Emergency assignments, impending deadlines, crises, or crucial exams.

     - Important but Not Urgent (Schedule):
       - Definition: Tasks in this quadrant are important for long-term goals but not necessarily time-sensitive. They should be scheduled and planned for.
       - Examples: Long-term projects, studying for upcoming exams (when there's ample time), personal development, and goal setting.

     - Urgent but Not Important (Delegate):
       - Definition: Tasks in this quadrant are urgent but not directly related to important goals. Adolescents may consider delegating or finding efficient ways to handle them.
       - Examples: Minor interruptions, routine administrative tasks, some emails or messages, and activities that may be urgent for others but not directly for the adolescent.

- Neither Urgent nor Important (Eliminate):
    - Definition: Tasks in this quadrant neither contribute to important goals nor have immediate urgency. Adolescents may choose to eliminate or minimize these tasks.
    - Examples: Unproductive activities, excessive social media browsing, time-wasting activities, or low-priority distractions.

2. **How Adolescents Can Use the Eisenhower Matrix:**

- **Task Assessment:**
    - Adolescents should start by listing all their tasks and assignments, both school-related and personal, in a comprehensive to-do list.

- **Categorization:**
    - Next, they can categorize each task by placing it in one of the four quadrants based on its importance and urgency. This requires careful consideration of each task's impact on their academic and personal goals.

- **Prioritization:**
    - Once tasks are categorized, adolescents can prioritize their work. Tasks in the "Urgent and Important" quadrant should be tackled first, followed by those in the "Important but Not Urgent" quadrant, which may require planning and scheduling. Tasks in the other two quadrants may be delegated or eliminated, freeing up valuable time.

- **Planning and Execution:**
    - Adolescents should create a daily or weekly schedule that reflects their prioritized tasks. They can use time management techniques like the Pomodoro Technique or task batching to allocate time for each category of tasks.

- **Regular Review:**
    - It's crucial to regularly review and update the Eisenhower Matrix as new tasks arise or priorities change. This ongoing assessment helps adolescents

stay adaptable and focused on their most critical goals.

The Eisenhower Matrix is a valuable tool for adolescents to optimize their time and effort. By categorizing tasks and systematically prioritizing them, they can ensure that their work aligns with their academic and personal objectives. This method not only enhances productivity but also reduces anxiety related to managing a hectic schedule and meeting deadlines.

- **Time Sensitivity:** Prioritizing tasks based on their time sensitivity helps adolescents meet deadlines without feeling rushed. They can also allocate more time and attention to tasks that require deeper focus.

Creating a Schedule:

Definition: *Creating a schedule involves organizing one's day, week, or month to allocate time for different activities, including academic work, relaxation, socializing, and self-care.*

- **Benefits for Anxiety:** A well-structured schedule provides adolescents with a sense of predictability and control, which can help reduce anxiety. It prevents last-minute rushes and minimizes the risk of feeling overwhelmed.

- **Time Blocks:** Adolescents can create a schedule using time blocks, allocating specific time slots for different tasks or activities. This includes study time, leisure time, exercise, and relaxation.

- **Flexibility:** While a schedule offers structure, it's essential to include flexibility for unexpected events or breaks. This flexibility allows adolescents to adapt to changing circumstances without feeling stressed.

Setting Realistic Goals:

Definition: *Setting realistic goals involves establishing achievable objectives within a given timeframe. Realistic goals are neither too easy nor too challenging, aligning with the adolescent's abilities and resources.*

- **Benefits for Anxiety:** Unrealistic goals can contribute to anxiety by creating undue pressure and fear of failure. Setting achievable goals promotes a sense of accomplishment and reduces stress.

- **SMART Goals:** Adolescents can use the SMART criteria to set goals that are:

  - Specific
  - Measurable
  - Achievable
  - Relevant
  - Time-bound

  This framework helps them clarify their objectives and create a plan to reach them.

- **Breaking Down Goals:** When tackling larger projects or long-term goals, adolescents can break them down into smaller, manageable steps. This makes the process less overwhelming and allows for a sense of progress along the way.

Avoiding Procrastination:

Definition: *Procrastination is the act of delaying or avoiding tasks that need to be accomplished. It often stems from anxiety, fear of failure, or a lack of motivation.*

- **Impact on Anxiety:** Procrastination can exacerbate anxiety because the impending tasks continue to loom in the background, causing ongoing stress. Overcoming procrastination can significantly reduce anxiety.

- **Procrastination Triggers:** Adolescents can identify their triggers for procrastination, which may include perfectionism, fear of judgment, or feeling overwhelmed. Recognizing these triggers is the first step in addressing them.

- **Time Management Techniques:** Adolescents can employ time management techniques to combat procrastination, such as the Pomodoro Technique (25 minutes of focused work followed by a

5-minute break), task batching (grouping similar tasks together), and setting timers or alarms.

1. The Pomodoro Technique:

    a. Description: The Pomodoro Technique is a time management method developed by Francesco Cirillo. It involves breaking work into intervals, traditionally 25 minutes in length, separated by short breaks. Each interval is referred to as a "Pomodoro," named after the tomato-shaped kitchen timer Cirillo used during college.

    b. Benefits for Adolescents: The Pomodoro Technique is particularly effective for adolescents dealing with anxiety and procrastination because it provides a structured approach to work. The short, focused intervals reduce the perceived effort and help them maintain concentration.

    c. How to Use It: Adolescents can set a timer for 25 minutes and work on a specific task or assignment with full concentration during that time. After the Pomodoro is complete, they take a 5-minute break to relax, stretch, or clear their mind. After completing four Pomodoros, they can take a longer break of 15-30 minutes.

    d. Adaptability: The Pomodoro Technique is highly adaptable. Adolescents can adjust the duration of Pomodoros to suit their needs, starting with shorter intervals if necessary and gradually increasing them as they build their concentration.

2. Task Batching:
    a. Description: Task batching involves grouping similar tasks or activities together and completing them in a designated block of time. This approach minimizes context switching, which can be a source of distraction and procrastination.

    b. Benefits for Adolescents: Adolescents often juggle multiple responsibilities, from schoolwork to extracurricular activities. Task batching helps them streamline their workflow by focusing on similar tasks at once, reducing mental clutter and enhancing efficiency.

c. How to Use It: Adolescents can categorize their tasks based on similarity or priority. For example, they can batch all their reading assignments, research tasks, or administrative work together. By dedicating specific time blocks to these tasks, they can work more efficiently and stay organized.

d. Flexibility: Task batching allows adolescents to create a customized schedule that aligns with their preferences and energy levels. They can allocate longer or shorter time blocks based on the complexity of the tasks.

3. Setting Timers or Alarms:

a. Description: Setting timers or alarms involves using time-tracking tools to allocate specific periods for tasks or activities. These reminders help adolescents stay on track and ensure they allocate appropriate time to each task.

b. Benefits for Adolescents: Timers and alarms provide a sense of structure and accountability. They serve as visual and auditory cues, prompting adolescents to start or switch tasks, reducing the likelihood of procrastination.

c. How to Use It: Adolescents can use timers or alarms on their smartphones, tablets, or computers to schedule work sessions or breaks. For instance, they can set a timer for 30 minutes to complete a math assignment and then take a 10-minute break before starting the next task.

d. Incremental Progress: Setting timers or alarms encourages adolescents to work incrementally, focusing on the task at hand for a specific duration. This approach is less intimidating than thinking about completing an entire assignment in one go.

These time management techniques offer practical tools for adolescents to overcome procrastination and manage their time more effectively. By implementing strategies like the Pomodoro Technique, task batching, and setting timers or alarms, they can enhance their concentration, productivity, and overall time management skills. This not only helps reduce anxiety related to deadlines and workload but also empowers them to take control of their responsibilities.

- **Self-Compassion:** Encourage adolescents to practice self-compassion when they do procrastinate. Instead of self-criticism, they can acknowledge their feelings, forgive themselves, and refocus on the task at hand.

Effective time management strategies empower adolescents to take control of their schedules and reduce anxiety. By prioritizing tasks, creating schedules, setting realistic goals, and addressing procrastination, they can enhance their productivity, build self-confidence, and ultimately manage anxiety more effectively.

Section 2: Test and Homework Anxiety

Test and homework anxiety are common challenges for students. This section provides insights into understanding and managing these anxieties:

- **Recognizing Test Anxiety**: Understand the symptoms and signs of test anxiety, which can include physical discomfort, racing thoughts, and decreased concentration.
- **Effective Study Strategies**: Learn study techniques that help reduce anxiety, including creating a study plan, practicing active recall, and using mnemonic devices.
- **Managing Homework Anxiety**: Explore strategies to manage anxiety related to homework, such as breaking assignments into smaller tasks and setting time limits.
- **Test-Taking Strategies**: Discover practical test-taking strategies, including relaxation techniques, time management during exams, and

staying focused.

Recognizing Test Anxiety:

Definition: *Test anxiety is a form of performance anxiety characterized by heightened stress and worry before or during exams. Recognizing the signs and symptoms of test anxiety is the first step in addressing it.*

- **Signs and Symptoms:**
    - Physical symptoms: These may include sweating, trembling, rapid heartbeat, nausea, or feeling lightheaded.

    - Cognitive symptoms: Test-anxious adolescents may experience racing thoughts, blanking out, or difficulty concentrating.

    - Emotional symptoms: Anxiety can lead to feelings of fear, apprehension, or even panic before or during tests.

    - Behavioral symptoms: Some adolescents may engage in avoidance behaviors, such as skipping exams or procrastinating on test preparation.

- **Effective Recognition Strategies:**
    - Self-awareness: Adolescents can learn to identify physical, cognitive, emotional, and behavioral signs of anxiety. Keeping a journal or diary can help them track these symptoms over time.

    - Regular self-assessment: Encourage adolescents to regularly assess their anxiety levels before, during, and after tests. This self-reflection can help them identify patterns and triggers.

Effective Study Strategies:

Definition: *Effective study strategies are techniques and approaches that enhance learning and retention of information. Adolescents can benefit from a variety of strategies tailored to their individual learning styles and needs.*

- **Examples of Effective Study Strategies:**
    - Active Engagement: Actively engage with study material by asking questions, summarizing key points, and teaching

concepts to others.

- Spaced Repetition: Distribute study sessions over time to improve long-term retention. Review material periodically rather than cramming.

- Use of Visual Aids: Create diagrams, mind maps, or flashcards to visualize complex concepts and aid memory recall.

- Practice Tests: Take practice exams or quizzes to simulate test conditions and identify areas that need further review.

- Peer Teaching: Explain concepts to peers or family members. Teaching others reinforces one's understanding of the material.

- Healthy Lifestyle: Maintain a balanced diet, regular exercise, and sufficient sleep to support cognitive function and reduce stress.

Managing Homework Anxiety:

Definition: *Homework anxiety refers to the stress and apprehension some adolescents experience when faced with assignments, projects, or homework tasks.*

- **Management Strategies:**
    - Break Tasks Into Smaller Steps: Encourage adolescents to break down assignments into smaller, manageable tasks. This approach prevents feeling overwhelmed and makes progress more tangible.

    - Time Management: Teach effective time management skills, such as creating a homework schedule, setting timers, and using the Pomodoro Technique to maintain focus.

    - Stress Reduction Techniques: Practice stress reduction techniques like deep breathing, mindfulness, or short breaks during homework sessions to manage anxiety.

    - Seeking Help: Adolescents should feel comfortable seeking help from teachers, parents, or tutors when they encounter challenging homework. It's important to promote a growth mindset, emphasizing that it's okay to ask for assistance.

Test-Taking Strategies:

Definition: *Test-taking strategies are techniques that adolescents can employ during exams to maximize their performance and reduce test anxiety.*

- **Examples of Test-Taking Strategies:**
    - Read Instructions Carefully: Start by thoroughly reading and understanding test instructions. This avoids misunderstandings and prevents errors.

    - Time Management: Allocate time wisely. Begin with easier questions, and if a question proves challenging, move on and return to it later.

    - Answer All Questions: Encourage adolescents to attempt all questions, even if they are unsure. In most cases, there is no penalty for guessing, and partial credit may be awarded.

    - Review and Proofread: If time permits, review answers for accuracy and clarity. Check for omitted questions and review written responses for errors.

    - Stay Calm: Teach stress-reduction techniques like deep breathing or focusing on a calming mantra to stay composed during the test.

By recognizing test anxiety, implementing effective study strategies, managing homework-related stress, and employing test-taking strategies, adolescents can enhance their academic performance and reduce anxiety associated with exams and assignments. These skills not only contribute to better grades but also build confidence and resilience in facing academic challenges.

Section 3: Seeking Help at School

Schools offer valuable resources and support for students dealing with anxiety. This section provides guidance on seeking help and support within the school environment:

- **School Counselors**: Understand the role of school counselors in providing emotional support, guidance, and referrals to additional resources.
- **Teacher Communication**: Learn effective ways to communicate with teachers about anxiety-related challenges, including requesting accommodations if needed.
- **Supportive Services**: Explore the range of supportive services available at school, such as tutoring, study groups, and access to educational accommodations.
- **Peer Support Groups**: Discover the benefits of joining peer support groups or clubs related to anxiety or mental health to connect with others facing similar challenges.

By the end of this chapter, you'll have a comprehensive understanding of time management strategies to reduce academic stress, techniques to cope with test and homework anxiety, and how to navigate the school environment to seek help and support, ultimately promoting academic success and well-being for teenagers.

School Counselors:

- **Role of School Counselors:** School counselors are trained professionals who play a crucial role in supporting the emotional, academic, and social development of adolescents. They can be a valuable resource for students dealing with anxiety.

- **Services Provided:**
    - Individual Counseling: School counselors offer one-on-one counseling sessions to address students' specific concerns, including anxiety. These sessions provide a safe and confidential space for adolescents to express their feelings and receive guidance.
    - Group Counseling: In addition to individual sessions, school counselors may facilitate group counseling sessions. These groups can focus on topics such as stress management, social

skills, or coping with anxiety, allowing adolescents to connect with peers facing similar challenges.
- Crisis Intervention: School counselors are trained to provide immediate support during crises, including situations involving severe anxiety or emotional distress.
- Academic Guidance: They can assist in course selection, academic planning, and college or career counseling, helping adolescents set and achieve their educational goals.

- **Regular Check-Ins:** Adolescents are encouraged to schedule regular check-ins with their school counselors, even when they're not facing immediate crises. These meetings can help students proactively address anxiety or stress.

Teacher Communication:

- **Importance of Communication:** Open and effective communication between adolescents and their teachers is vital for recognizing and addressing anxiety-related challenges.

- **Establishing Communication Channels:**
    - Adolescents should be encouraged to establish communication channels with their teachers, which can include in-person discussions, email, or online platforms used for school communication.
    - Teachers can play a proactive role by creating a classroom environment that welcomes questions and concerns from students.

- **Sharing Anxiety Challenges:** Adolescents should feel comfortable discussing their anxiety challenges with their teachers. Teachers can provide support, accommodations, or resources to help students succeed academically while managing anxiety.

- **Collaboration:** Collaboration between teachers, school counselors, and parents can ensure a coordinated approach to addressing a student's anxiety. Regular communication can help identify early signs of anxiety-related difficulties.

Supportive Services:

Definition: *Supportive services encompass a range of resources and accommodations provided by schools to help adolescents manage anxiety and succeed academically.*

- **Examples of Supportive Services:**
    - Academic Accommodations: Schools may offer accommodations such as extended test-taking time, quiet testing environments, or the use of assistive technology for students with anxiety-related difficulties.
    - Study Skills Workshops: Workshops on study skills, time management, and stress reduction can be offered to equip adolescents with tools to manage their academic workload effectively.
    - Mental Health Programs: Schools can implement mental health awareness programs and provide access to mental health professionals who can support students with anxiety disorders.
    - Emotional Support Animals: In some cases, schools may allow registered emotional support animals to accompany students, providing comfort and reducing anxiety.

- **Individualized Education Plans (IEPs) and 504 Plans**: Adolescents with diagnosed anxiety disorders may be eligible for an IEP or a 504 plan, which outlines specific accommodations and support tailored to their needs.

Peer Support Groups:

Definition: *Peer support groups are structured settings where adolescents with similar challenges, including anxiety, come together to share experiences, coping strategies, and emotional support.*

- **Benefits:**
    - Peer support groups create a sense of belonging and reduce feelings of isolation for adolescents dealing with anxiety.
    - They offer a safe space to express thoughts and feelings without judgment.
    - Adolescents can learn from peers who have successfully managed anxiety and implemented effective coping strategies.

- ○ Group discussions and activities can enhance social skills and self-confidence.

- **Facilitation:** Peer support groups are often facilitated by trained professionals, such as school counselors or mental health specialists, who ensure the group remains a supportive and constructive environment.

Support systems within the school environment, including school counselors, teacher communication, supportive services, and peer support groups, are instrumental in helping adolescents manage anxiety and thrive academically. These resources contribute to a holistic approach to well-being, fostering resilience and emotional growth in students.

Chapter 14: The Role of Technology in Anxiety Relief

The digital world offers both opportunities and challenges for teenagers dealing with anxiety. This chapter explores the use of apps and online resources for anxiety management, the benefits of virtual support groups, and the importance of practicing digital detox to maintain a healthy balance.

Section 1: Apps and Online Resources

Technology can be a valuable tool for managing anxiety when used mindfully. This section explores apps and online resources that can assist teenagers in their anxiety management journey:

- **Anxiety-Tracking Apps**: Discover apps designed to help users track their anxiety symptoms, triggers, and progress over time.
- **Mindfulness and Meditation Apps**: Explore mindfulness and meditation apps that offer guided practices and relaxation techniques to reduce anxiety.
- **Educational Websites**: Learn about reputable websites that provide information, articles, and resources on anxiety and mental health.
- **Online Therapy Platforms**: Understand the benefits of online therapy platforms, which offer access to licensed therapists through video or text-based sessions.

Anxiety-Tracking Apps:

- **Purpose:** Anxiety-tracking apps are designed to help adolescents monitor their anxiety symptoms, triggers, and patterns over time. These apps promote self-awareness and provide valuable insights into their emotional well-being.

- **Key Features:**
  - Symptom Tracking: Adolescents can record their anxiety symptoms, such as racing thoughts, rapid heartbeat, or irritability, on a daily or as-needed basis.

- ○ Triggers Identification: These apps allow users to identify and log specific triggers or stressors that contribute to their anxiety, such as exams, social situations, or family issues.
- ○ Progress Tracking: Over time, adolescents can track their progress, recognizing improvements or patterns that may require intervention.
- ○ Goal Setting: Some apps enable users to set goals for managing anxiety and offer reminders to practice anxiety-reducing techniques.

- **Examples of Anxiety-Tracking Apps:** Notable apps in this category include "MoodTools," "Daylio," and "eMoods," which provide comprehensive tools for monitoring emotional well-being.

Mindfulness and Meditation Apps:

- **Purpose:** Mindfulness and meditation apps are designed to teach adolescents relaxation techniques, mindfulness practices, and meditation exercises to reduce anxiety and stress.

- **Key Features:**
  - ○ Guided Sessions: These apps offer guided meditation and mindfulness sessions led by experienced instructors.
  - ○ Breathing Exercises: Breathing techniques to calm the mind and reduce physical tension are often included.
  - ○ Progressive Relaxation: Some apps incorporate progressive muscle relaxation exercises to release physical tension.
  - ○ Daily Mindfulness Practices: Adolescents can engage in short daily mindfulness exercises to build a consistent practice.

- **Examples of Mindfulness and Meditation Apps:** Well-known apps include "Headspace," "Calm," and "Insight Timer," which provide a variety of mindfulness and meditation resources suitable for adolescents.

Educational Websites:

- **Purpose:** Educational websites offer valuable information and resources to help adolescents understand anxiety, stress management, and coping strategies.

- **Key Features:**

- o Articles and Guides: These websites provide informative articles, guides, and blog posts on anxiety, its causes, symptoms, and strategies for managing it.
- o Interactive Tools: Some educational websites offer interactive tools and quizzes to help adolescents assess their stress levels and learn about coping techniques.
- o Video Content: Educational websites may include video content, such as webinars or interviews with mental health experts, providing valuable insights.
- o Community Forums: Some websites offer discussion forums where adolescents can connect with others facing similar challenges, fostering a sense of community and support.

- **Examples of Educational Websites**: Well-regarded educational websites include the Anxiety and Depression Association of America (ADAA) website, which offers a wealth of resources, and the National Institute of Mental Health (NIMH) website, which provides information on mental health topics.

Online Therapy Platforms:

- **Purpose:** Online therapy platforms connect adolescents with licensed mental health professionals who can provide therapy and support for managing anxiety and stress through virtual sessions.

- **Key Features:**
    - o Access to Therapists: These platforms offer access to a network of licensed therapists, counselors, and psychologists who specialize in treating anxiety and related conditions.
    - o Flexible Scheduling: Adolescents can typically schedule therapy sessions at times that are convenient for them, reducing scheduling conflicts with school and other commitments.
    - o Secure Communication: Online therapy platforms ensure secure and confidential communication between the adolescent and therapist.
    - o **Various Modalities:** Therapy can be conducted through video calls, phone calls, or text-based messaging, allowing adolescents to choose the modality that suits them best.

- **Examples of Online Therapy Platforms:** Prominent platforms include "BetterHelp," "Talkspace," and "Therapy for Black Girls," which offer accessible and confidential therapy services for adolescents.

These online resources and apps provide adolescents with valuable tools and support to manage anxiety and stress in a digital age. When used mindfully and in conjunction with other support systems, they can contribute to enhanced emotional well-being and resilience. However, it's essential to encourage adolescents to seek professional help if their anxiety symptoms persist or worsen.

Section 2: Virtual Support Groups

Connecting with others who share similar experiences can be empowering for teenagers dealing with anxiety. This section explores the advantages of virtual support groups:

- **Peer Support Networks**: Learn about online communities and forums where teenagers can connect with peers facing similar anxiety challenges.
- **Online Support Groups**: Discover the benefits of joining virtual support groups moderated by mental health professionals, which provide a safe space for sharing and learning.
- **Specialized Groups**: Explore the availability of virtual support groups tailored to specific anxiety disorders, such as social anxiety or generalized anxiety disorder.
- **Anonymity and Accessibility**: Understand how virtual support groups offer anonymity and accessibility, making it easier for teenagers to seek support without the fear of judgment.

Peer Support Networks:

Definition: Peer support networks are informal groups of individuals who share similar experiences or challenges, such as anxiety, and come together to provide mutual emotional support and encouragement.

- **Characteristics:**
    - Shared Experiences: Members of peer support networks often have firsthand experience with anxiety, making them empathetic and understanding allies.

- o Informal Setting: These networks typically operate in a casual and non-clinical environment, creating a comfortable atmosphere for sharing.
- o Emotional Support: Adolescents in peer support networks can openly discuss their feelings, fears, and coping strategies with others who can relate.
- o Validation: Peer support networks offer validation and reassurance, helping adolescents feel less isolated in their experiences.

- **Benefits:**

  - o Reduced Isolation: Adolescents with anxiety often feel isolated. Peer support networks can combat this isolation by connecting them with others who face similar challenges.
  - o Empowerment: Sharing successes and coping strategies with peers can empower adolescents to take an active role in managing their anxiety.
  - o Sense of Belonging: These networks foster a sense of belonging and acceptance, which can boost self-esteem and resilience.

Online Support Groups:

Definition: *Online support groups are virtual communities where individuals with shared concerns, such as anxiety, come together to exchange experiences, advice, and emotional support through online platforms and forums.*

- **Characteristics:**

  - o Accessibility: Online support groups are accessible to adolescents regardless of their location, providing a broader reach than in-person groups.
  - o Diverse Membership: These groups can attract participants from various backgrounds, offering diverse perspectives and insights.
  - o Privacy: Adolescents can participate anonymously, which can be particularly appealing for those who are hesitant to disclose their identity.
  - o Moderation: Many online support groups are moderated to ensure respectful and supportive interactions.

- **Benefits:**

    - Global Reach: Adolescents can connect with individuals worldwide who share their experiences, widening their support network.
    - 24/7 Availability: Online support groups are available around the clock, providing support whenever it's needed.
    - Anonymity: Anonymity can encourage more open and honest sharing of thoughts and feelings.

Specialized Groups:

Definition: *Specialized support groups cater to specific demographics or conditions within the broader context of anxiety, addressing unique challenges faced by certain groups of adolescents.*

- **Examples:**

    - Gender-Based Groups: Some specialized groups may focus on the unique experiences of boys or girls dealing with anxiety.
    - Cultural or Ethnic Groups: These groups provide a space for adolescents from particular cultural or ethnic backgrounds to discuss anxiety within their cultural context.
    - LGBTQ+ Support: Specialized groups may cater to LGBTQ+ adolescents, who may have distinct anxiety-related concerns.
    - Age-Related Groups: Some support groups are tailored to specific age groups, such as middle school or high school students.

- **Benefits:**

    - Tailored Support: Specialized groups offer support and resources specifically tailored to the needs and experiences of their members.
    - Enhanced Comfort: Adolescents may feel more comfortable sharing their challenges and seeking advice from peers who have similar backgrounds or identities.

Anonymity and Accessibility:
- **Advantages of Anonymity:**

- o Adolescents, especially those concerned about stigma or judgment, can participate anonymously in online support groups or specialized networks, promoting open and honest discussions.
  - o Anonymity can reduce self-consciousness, allowing adolescents to express their thoughts and feelings more freely.
  - o It removes geographical barriers, enabling individuals to connect with peers from diverse backgrounds.

- **Advantages of Accessibility:**
  - o Online support networks and groups are accessible from anywhere with an internet connection, eliminating geographical limitations.
  - o Adolescents can access these resources at their convenience, fitting them into their schedules.
    - Accessibility promotes inclusivity, ensuring that adolescents with physical or social constraints can still find valuable support.

Incorporating these support networks into an adolescent's journey in managing anxiety can enhance their emotional well-being and resilience. Adolescents should be encouraged to explore different options and find the support system that best aligns with their needs and preferences.

Section 3: Digital Detox

While technology can be a valuable resource, it's essential to maintain a healthy balance with the digital world. This section emphasizes the importance of digital detox:

- **Recognizing Digital Overload**: Understand the signs of digital overload, such as increased anxiety, decreased sleep quality, and reduced face-to-face interactions.
- **Setting Boundaries**: Learn how to establish clear boundaries around technology use, including designated tech-free times and spaces.
- **Engaging in Offline Activities**: Discover the benefits of engaging in offline activities, such as hobbies, sports, and spending quality time with loved ones.

- **Practicing Mindful Tech Use**: Understand the concept of mindful tech use, which involves using technology intentionally and consciously to enhance well-being.

By the end of this chapter, you'll have insights into the role of apps and online resources in anxiety management, the benefits of virtual support groups, and the importance of maintaining a healthy balance with the digital world through practices like digital detox.

Recognizing Digital Overload:

Definition: Digital overload, also known as screen overload or digital overwhelm, occurs when adolescents spend excessive time using digital devices, such as smartphones, tablets, or computers, to the detriment of their well-being.

- **Signs and Symptoms:**
    - Increased Anxiety: Spending too much time online can lead to heightened anxiety, as adolescents may encounter stressful content or feel pressured by social media.
    - Reduced Focus: Digital overload can lead to difficulty concentrating on tasks and reduced productivity in schoolwork or other activities.
    - Physical Health Issues: Excessive screen time can contribute to physical health problems, including eyestrain, headaches, and disrupted sleep patterns.
    - Neglected Responsibilities: Adolescents may neglect responsibilities, such as schoolwork, chores, or face-to-face social interactions, in favor of online activities.

- **Recognizing the Impact:** Adolescents should be educated about the potential negative consequences of digital overload to help them recognize when their technology use is affecting their well-being.

Setting Boundaries:

- **Importance of Boundaries:** Establishing clear boundaries around technology use is essential for promoting a healthy balance between online and offline life.

- **Tips for Setting Boundaries:**

- Screen-Free Zones: Designate certain areas in the home, such as the dining room or bedrooms, as screen-free zones to encourage face-to-face interactions and relaxation.
- Scheduled Tech Time: Implement set periods for technology use, such as designated hours for homework, social media, or entertainment.
- Digital Detox Days: Encourage adolescents to take regular digital detox days or weekends to unplug from screens and engage in offline activities.
- Device-Free Meals: Promote the practice of having device-free meals with family and friends to foster meaningful conversations.

- **Consistent Communication:** Parents and caregivers should maintain open and consistent communication with adolescents about the importance of setting boundaries and respecting screen time limits.

Engaging in Offline Activities:

- **Benefits of Offline Activities:** Engaging in offline activities provides adolescents with opportunities to disconnect from screens, reduce stress, and develop various skills and interests.

- **Examples of Offline Activities:**
  - Physical Exercise: Encourage adolescents to participate in physical activities like sports, yoga, or hiking to promote physical and mental well-being.

  - Creative Hobbies: Support the development of creative hobbies such as painting, writing, playing musical instruments, or crafting.

  - Face-to-Face Socializing: Adolescents should be encouraged to spend quality time with friends and family through face-to-face interactions, which are essential for building and maintaining relationships.
  - Nature and Outdoors: Spending time in nature, whether through hiking, camping, or simply enjoying a walk in the park, can have a calming and grounding effect.

- **Balanced Lifestyle:** Promote a balanced lifestyle that includes a mix of technology use and offline activities to help adolescents achieve overall well-being.

Practicing Mindful Tech Use:

Definition: Mindful tech use involves being intentional and aware of how technology is used to support well-being rather than detract from it.

- **Tips for Mindful Tech Use:**
    - Tech-Free Wind-Down: Encourage adolescents to establish tech-free wind-down routines before bedtime to improve sleep quality.
    - Screen Time Tracking: Use apps or built-in screen time tracking features on devices to monitor and limit daily screen time.
    - Mindful Social Media Use: Teach adolescents to critically evaluate their social media use and its impact on their self-esteem and mental health.
    - Digital Sabbaticals: Periodically taking a break from social media or other digital platforms can help adolescents refresh and refocus.

- **Digital Literacy:** Empower adolescents with digital literacy skills, including media literacy, online etiquette, and critical thinking about the content they consume.

By recognizing digital overload, setting boundaries, engaging in offline activities, and practicing mindful tech use, adolescents can achieve a healthier balance between their digital and offline lives. These strategies contribute to reduced anxiety and improved overall well-being, ensuring that technology serves as a valuable tool rather than a source of stress.

Chapter 15: Overcoming Social Anxiety

Social anxiety can be particularly challenging for teenagers. This chapter provides insights into understanding social anxiety, offers practical tips for handling social situations, and explores gradual exposure as an effective approach to managing social anxiety.

Section 1: Understanding Social Anxiety

Social anxiety often involves intense fear and self-consciousness in social situations. This section delves into the nature of social anxiety:

- **Defining Social Anxiety**: Understand what social anxiety is, including its symptoms and how it differs from shyness.
- **Common Triggers**: Explore common triggers for social anxiety, such as public speaking, meeting new people, or being the center of attention.
- **Physical and Emotional Responses**: Recognize the physical and emotional responses associated with social anxiety, including blushing, sweating, and irrational fears of judgment.
- **Impact on Daily Life**: Learn how social anxiety can affect various aspects of a teenager's life, from academic performance to social relationships.

Defining Social Anxiety:

Definition: *Social anxiety, also known as social phobia, is a mental health condition characterized by intense fear, anxiety, and self-consciousness in social situations. Individuals with social anxiety often have a strong fear of negative judgment, embarrassment, or humiliation by others.*

- **Key Characteristics:**
    - Excessive Worry: Those with social anxiety excessively worry about being judged or negatively evaluated by peers or strangers.

- Avoidance Behavior: Socially anxious individuals may engage in avoidance behavior, avoiding social situations or enduring them with extreme discomfort.
- Physical Symptoms: Anxiety in social situations can trigger physical symptoms such as sweating, trembling, blushing, or a racing heart.
- Interference with Functioning: Social anxiety can significantly interfere with a person's ability to engage in daily activities, form relationships, and pursue goals.

- **Duration and Diagnosis:** Social anxiety disorder is diagnosed when these symptoms persist for at least six months and significantly disrupt daily life.

Common Triggers:

- **Performance Situations:** Social anxiety often intensifies in performance situations, such as public speaking, giving presentations, or performing in front of others.

- **Social Interactions:** Everyday social interactions, including making small talk, meeting new people, or attending social gatherings, can trigger social anxiety.

- **Authority Figures:** Some individuals may experience heightened anxiety around authority figures or people they perceive as judgmental.

- **Evaluative Situations:** Being evaluated or scrutinized, whether in academic, professional, or personal contexts, can be particularly anxiety-inducing for those with social anxiety.

- **Personal Variation:** Triggers can vary from person to person, and what causes anxiety for one individual may not have the same effect on another. Identifying personal triggers is an important step in managing social anxiety.

Physical and Emotional Responses:

- **Physical Responses**:
  - Sweating: Increased sweating, especially on the palms or forehead, is a common physical response to social anxiety.

- ○ Trembling or Shaking: Individuals with social anxiety may experience trembling or shaking in their hands or other parts of their body.
- ○ Rapid Heartbeat: Anxiety in social situations can lead to an elevated heart rate, which may be physically uncomfortable.
- ○ Nausea or Upset Stomach: Some people experience gastrointestinal symptoms, including nausea or an upset stomach, due to social anxiety.

- **Emotional Responses:**
  - ○ Intense Fear: Social anxiety is characterized by intense fear of judgment, criticism, or rejection by others.
  - ○ Self-Consciousness: Those with social anxiety often feel excessively self-conscious, focusing on their perceived flaws or shortcomings.
  - ○ Negative Self-Talk: Individuals may engage in negative self-talk, believing that others are thinking negatively about them.
  - ○ Avoidance: Emotional responses often lead to avoidance behavior, where individuals actively avoid or withdraw from social situations to minimize distress.

Impact on Daily Life:

- **Academic Performance:** Social anxiety can hinder academic performance, especially in situations requiring class participation, oral presentations, or group projects.

- **Career and Professional Growth:** It can limit career opportunities and professional growth, as networking, job interviews, and workplace interactions become sources of anxiety.

- **Relationships:** Social anxiety can strain personal relationships, making it challenging to form and maintain connections.

- **Quality of Life:** Overall, social anxiety can significantly reduce an individual's quality of life, as it affects their ability to engage in a wide range of social and professional activities.

- **Isolation:** To avoid the distress associated with social situations, some individuals with social anxiety may isolate themselves, which can exacerbate feelings of loneliness and depression.

Recognizing social anxiety, understanding common triggers, and being aware of physical and emotional responses is the first step in seeking support and treatment. Early intervention, including therapy and cognitive-behavioral techniques, can help individuals with social anxiety manage their symptoms and lead more fulfilling lives.

Section 2: Tips for Social Situations

Effective strategies can help teenagers navigate social situations with greater confidence. This section provides practical tips for handling social anxiety:

- **Preparation**: Understand the value of preparation, whether for a social event, a presentation, or a conversation, in reducing anxiety.
- **Mindfulness and Self-Compassion**: Learn how mindfulness and self-compassion techniques can help manage self-critical thoughts and reduce anxiety.
- **Communication Skills**: Explore strategies for improving communication skills, including active listening and assertiveness, to foster better social interactions.
- **Positive Self-Talk**: Understand the importance of positive self-talk and how it can counter negative thoughts and boost self-esteem.

Preparation:

- **Thorough Preparation:** Adequate preparation is a crucial component in managing performance anxiety. Whether it's a presentation, test, or extracurricular activity, thorough preparation can boost confidence and reduce anxiety.

- **Practice and Rehearsal:** Repeatedly practicing the task or activity can help individuals become more comfortable and proficient, reducing the fear of making mistakes.

- **Simulate the Environment:** Whenever possible, simulate the performance environment. For example, if it's a presentation, practice in front of a small group of friends or family to mimic the experience of presenting to an audience.

- **Time Management:** Plan a schedule that allows for a balanced amount of study or preparation time. Avoid last-minute cramming, which can increase anxiety.

Mindfulness and Self-Compassion:

- **Mindfulness Practices:** Engaging in mindfulness exercises, such as deep breathing or meditation, can help individuals stay present and manage anxious thoughts.

- **Self-Compassion:** Encourage individuals to treat themselves with the same kindness and understanding they would offer to a friend. Self-compassion involves acknowledging one's feelings without self-criticism.

- **Positive Self-Image:** Remind individuals that it's normal to have imperfections and make mistakes. Accepting oneself as imperfect can reduce the fear of judgment.

- **Grounding Techniques:** Teach grounding techniques, such as focusing on the five senses or using a grounding object, to help individuals stay connected to the present moment.

Communication Skills:

- **Active Listening:** Encourage individuals to practice active listening when engaging in conversations or presentations. This involves giving full attention to the speaker and responding thoughtfully.

- **Assertiveness:** Teach assertiveness skills to express thoughts, feelings, and needs effectively while respecting the rights of others. Being assertive can reduce anxiety related to communication.

- **Body Language:** Help individuals become aware of their body language. Maintaining good posture and using open and relaxed body language can convey confidence.

- **Public Speaking Training:** For public speaking anxiety, consider enrolling in public speaking or communication courses to develop effective speaking skills.

Positive Self-Talk:

- **Identify Negative Self-Talk:** Encourage individuals to recognize negative or self-critical thoughts when they arise. These thoughts can heighten anxiety.

- **Challenge Negative Thoughts:** Teach individuals to challenge and reframe negative self-talk. For example, if they think, "I'm going to mess up," they can reframe it as, "I'll do my best, and that's enough."

- **Affirmations:** Suggest the use of positive affirmations or mantras. These are short, positive statements individuals can repeat to themselves to boost confidence.

- **Visualization:** Visualization techniques involve mentally rehearsing a successful performance. It can reduce anxiety and increase self-assurance.

These strategies can be tailored to the specific context in which an individual experiences performance anxiety, whether it's related to public speaking, academic tests, or extracurricular activities. By implementing these techniques, individuals can develop resilience in the face of performance anxiety and improve their overall confidence and well-being.

Section 3: Gradual Exposure

Gradual exposure is a evidence-based technique for managing social anxiety. This section explains how gradual exposure works and how to implement it effectively:

- **What is Gradual Exposure?**: Define gradual exposure as a therapeutic technique that involves facing feared social situations in a systematic and gradual manner.
- **Creating a Hierarchy**: Learn how to create a hierarchy of social situations, starting with less anxiety-provoking scenarios and progressing to more challenging ones.

- **Exposure Exercises**: Explore specific exposure exercises for social anxiety, such as speaking in front of a mirror, initiating small talk, or attending group activities.
- **Tracking Progress**: Understand the importance of tracking progress and celebrating successes as you gradually confront and overcome social anxiety triggers.

By the end of this chapter, you'll have a comprehensive understanding of social anxiety, practical tips for navigating social situations with confidence, and insights into the effective use of gradual exposure as a tool for managing social anxiety in teenagers.

What is Gradual Exposure?:

Definition: *Gradual exposure, also known as systematic desensitization, is a therapeutic technique used to treat anxiety disorders, including phobias and social anxiety. It involves exposing individuals to feared situations or stimuli in a controlled and systematic manner, starting with less anxiety-provoking scenarios and progressing to more challenging ones.*

- **Principle:** Gradual exposure is based on the principle of habituation, which means that with repeated and controlled exposure to anxiety triggers, individuals can become desensitized to them over time. This can lead to a reduction in anxiety and fear responses.

- **Safe Environment:** Exposure exercises are typically conducted in a safe and supportive environment, often under the guidance of a therapist or mental health professional.

Creating a Hierarchy:

- **Hierarchy Development**: The first step in gradual exposure is to create an exposure hierarchy. This is a structured list of anxiety-inducing situations or stimuli related to the individual's specific fear or phobia.

- **Ranking Anxiety**: Each item on the hierarchy is ranked in order of anxiety or fear level, with the least anxiety-provoking situations at the bottom and the most anxiety-inducing ones at the top.

- **Tailored to Individual:** The hierarchy is tailored to the individual's unique fears and triggers. For example, in the case of social anxiety, it might include situations like making a phone call, attending a small gathering, or giving a presentation.

Exposure Exercises:

- **Progressive Exposure:** Once the hierarchy is established, exposure exercises are conducted in a progressive manner, starting with the least anxiety-provoking situation.

- **Controlled Exposure:** The individual is exposed to the feared situation or stimulus in a controlled and structured way. This exposure can be in vivo (real-life) or imaginal (imagining the situation).

- **Sensory Details:** During exposure, individuals are encouraged to pay attention to sensory details, thoughts, and physical sensations they experience. This helps them become more aware of their reactions.

- **Stay Until Anxiety Reduces:** Exposure exercises typically involve staying in the situation or engaging with the stimulus until the anxiety reduces or habituation occurs. This process can take time and may require several repetitions.

Tracking Progress:

- **Self-Monitoring:** Individuals are often encouraged to keep a record of their exposure experiences, noting the date, situation, anxiety level (e.g., on a scale from 1 to 10), and any observations or changes in their reactions.

- **Progression Up the Hierarchy:** As individuals successfully complete exposure exercises and habituate to lower-level anxiety situations, they can progress up the hierarchy to more challenging situations.

- **Celebrating Achievements:** Celebrating small achievements and milestones in exposure therapy can be motivating and reinforce progress.

- **Adjusting the Hierarchy:** The hierarchy may be adjusted over time based on the individual's progress and changing anxiety triggers.

Gradual exposure is an evidence-based technique used in cognitive-behavioral therapy (CBT) to help individuals confront and overcome their fears and anxieties. When conducted systematically and with proper guidance, it can be an effective approach for reducing anxiety and phobias, allowing individuals to regain control over their lives and build resilience in the face of anxiety-inducing situations.

Chapter 16: Managing Performance Anxiety

Performance anxiety can be a significant challenge for teenagers. This chapter provides insights into managing various forms of performance anxiety, including public speaking anxiety, test anxiety, and anxiety related to extracurricular activities.

Section 1: Public Speaking Anxiety

Public speaking anxiety can affect teenagers in academic and social contexts. In this section, we explore strategies for managing the fear of speaking in public:

- **Understanding Public Speaking Anxiety**: Define public speaking anxiety and its common symptoms, such as trembling, racing thoughts, and fear of judgment.
- **Preparation and Practice**: Learn effective techniques for preparing and practicing speeches, presentations, or class discussions to boost confidence.
- **Coping Strategies**: Explore coping strategies like controlled breathing, positive visualization, and reframing negative thoughts to reduce anxiety during public speaking.
- **Gradual Exposure**: Understand how gradual exposure can help teenagers desensitize themselves to the fear of public speaking over time.

Understanding Public Speaking Anxiety:

- **Definition and Prevalence:** Public speaking anxiety, often referred to as glossophobia, is a common form of performance anxiety characterized by a fear or apprehension of speaking in front of an audience. It's estimated that as much as 75% of the population experiences some level of anxiety about public speaking at some point in their lives.

- **Physical and Psychological Responses**: When faced with public speaking, individuals with this type of anxiety may experience a range of physical responses such as sweating, trembling, a racing heart, dry mouth, and muscle tension. Psychologically, they may suffer from racing thoughts, negative self-talk, and an inability to focus.

- **Causes and Triggers:** Public speaking anxiety can have various causes, including a fear of judgment or criticism, past negative experiences, low self-esteem, or a lack of confidence in one's speaking abilities. Common triggers include speaking in front of a large audience, giving a presentation, or participating in a public debate.

- **Impact on Daily Life:** The fear of public speaking can significantly impact one's personal and professional life. It can limit career opportunities, hinder academic success, and lead to avoidance of social situations that involve speaking in public.

Preparation and Practice:

- **Importance of Preparation:** Adequate preparation is essential for managing public speaking anxiety. Knowing your material thoroughly not only boosts your confidence but also ensures you can handle unexpected questions or challenges.

- **Rehearsal:** Rehearse your speech or presentation multiple times. Practice in front of a mirror, record yourself, or present to friends or family members to gain feedback.

- **Visualize Success:** Visualization is a powerful technique. Close your eyes and vividly imagine yourself speaking confidently and effectively in front of your audience. Visualizing success can reduce anxiety and boost self-assurance.

- **Familiarize with the Venue:** If possible, visit the venue where you'll be speaking ahead of time. Familiarity with the environment can ease anxiety on the day of the presentation.

Coping Strategies:

- **Deep Breathing:** Deep breathing exercises can help calm the nervous system. Practice diaphragmatic breathing by inhaling deeply through your nose, holding for a few seconds, and exhaling slowly through your mouth.

- **Positive Self-Talk:** Challenge negative thoughts with positive affirmations. Replace self-doubt with statements like, "I am well-prepared," "I have valuable insights to share," or "I can handle this."

- **Mindfulness:** Practicing mindfulness techniques, such as focusing on your breath or grounding exercises, can help keep you present and reduce anxiety about past or future events.

- **Seek Support:** Don't hesitate to seek support from a therapist or counselor if your public speaking anxiety is severely impacting your life. Therapists can provide strategies and exposure therapy to help you overcome your fear.

Gradual Exposure:

Definition: *Gradual exposure, also known as systematic desensitization, is a therapeutic approach for overcoming anxiety by gradually facing feared situations or stimuli.*

- **Application to Public Speaking Anxiety:** In the context of public speaking, gradual exposure involves progressively confronting speaking situations starting with less anxiety-inducing scenarios and advancing to more challenging ones.

- **Example Hierarchy:** Create a hierarchy of speaking situations ranked by anxiety level. This might start with speaking in front of a mirror, then to a small group of friends, followed by a larger group, and eventually to a public audience.

- **Desensitization Process:** The goal of gradual exposure is desensitization. By repeatedly and systematically exposing yourself to public speaking, you become less sensitive to the anxiety triggers, and your fear diminishes over time.

By understanding public speaking anxiety, adequately preparing and practicing, employing coping strategies, and considering gradual exposure, individuals can manage and eventually overcome their fear of public speaking, unlocking new opportunities for personal and professional growth.

Section 2: Test Anxiety

Test anxiety can hinder academic performance and increase stress. This section provides guidance on managing test anxiety:

- **Recognizing Test Anxiety**: Understand the symptoms of test anxiety, including physical discomfort, difficulty concentrating, and blanking out during exams.
- **Test Preparation Techniques**: Explore effective test preparation techniques, such as creating study schedules, practicing self-assessment, and using relaxation exercises.
- **Test-Taking Strategies**: Learn strategies for staying calm and focused during tests, including time management, mindfulness techniques, and positive self-talk.
- **Seeking Academic Support**: Discover how to seek academic support from teachers, counselors, or tutors when dealing with test anxiety.

Recognizing Test Anxiety:

- **Definition and Symptoms**: Test anxiety is a form of performance anxiety characterized by heightened fear or stress before, during, or after taking an exam or test. Recognizing test anxiety involves being aware of its common symptoms, which can include sweating, trembling, a racing heart, nausea, blanking out, difficulty concentrating, and negative thoughts about one's performance.

- **Physical and Cognitive Effects:** Test anxiety can lead to physical effects like muscle tension, headaches, and gastrointestinal discomfort. It can also result in cognitive effects such as self-doubt, fear of failure, and difficulty recalling information.

- **Impact on Performance:** Severe test anxiety can significantly impair test performance, causing individuals to perform below their actual knowledge and capabilities.

Test Preparation Techniques:

- **Effective Study Habits:** Establishing effective study habits is crucial for managing test anxiety. This includes setting a study schedule, creating a study plan, and breaking down the material into manageable segments.

- **Practice Tests:** Taking practice tests under conditions that mimic the real exam environment can help individuals become more comfortable with the testing process and reduce anxiety.

- **Active Learning Strategies:** Implement active learning strategies such as summarizing information, creating flashcards, or teaching the material to someone else. Active engagement with the material enhances retention and confidence.

- **Time Management:** Proper time management ensures that individuals have adequate time to cover all necessary topics without feeling rushed or overwhelmed.

Test-Taking Strategies:

- **Test-Day Preparation**: On the day of the test, ensure you are well-rested, have eaten a balanced meal, and arrive early to the testing venue. Avoid last-minute cramming, as it can increase anxiety.

- **Reading Instructions:** Carefully read all test instructions and questions. Misinterpreting instructions can lead to unnecessary stress.

- **Budgeting Time**: Allocate time wisely to each section or question. Skip difficult questions initially and return to them later if needed.

- **Mindful Breathing:** During the test, practice deep breathing exercises to stay calm. Inhale deeply through your nose, hold for a few seconds, and exhale slowly through your mouth.

Seeking Academic Support:

- **Tutoring and Academic Assistance:** If certain topics or concepts are causing anxiety, consider seeking tutoring or academic assistance. Tutors can provide personalized help to enhance understanding.

- **Study Groups:** Joining or forming study groups can be beneficial. Collaborative learning allows individuals to discuss and clarify doubts, reducing anxiety.

- **Counseling Services:** Many educational institutions offer counseling services where students can seek help for test anxiety. Counselors can provide strategies, counseling sessions, or referrals for further assistance.

- **Accommodations:** If test anxiety is a documented disability, students may be eligible for accommodations, such as extended time or a distraction-free testing environment. It's essential to communicate with disability services to explore these options.

Recognizing, preparing for, and managing test anxiety involves a combination of psychological strategies, effective study habits, and seeking academic support when needed. By addressing test anxiety proactively, individuals can improve their test performance and overall academic experience.

Section 3: Performance Anxiety in Extracurricular Activities

Extracurricular activities can be sources of both enjoyment and anxiety. This section explores ways to manage performance anxiety in extracurricular pursuits:

- **Identifying Anxiety Triggers**: Recognize the specific triggers of anxiety in extracurricular activities, whether it's a sports competition, a music performance, or a debate tournament.
- **Goal Setting**: Learn how setting realistic goals and focusing on personal growth can reduce performance-related stress.
- **Mindful Performance**: Understand the role of mindfulness and being present in the moment during extracurricular activities to alleviate anxiety.
- **Building Resilience**: Explore strategies for building resilience in the face of performance anxiety, including seeking support, learning from setbacks, and maintaining a growth mindset.

Identifying Anxiety Triggers:

- **Understanding Triggers:** Identifying anxiety triggers is the first step in managing performance anxiety. Triggers can be specific situations, events, or even thoughts that elicit anxiety. By recognizing these triggers, individuals can develop strategies to cope with them.

- **Common Triggers:** Common performance anxiety triggers include fear of failure, fear of judgment or criticism, pressure to meet high expectations (self-imposed or external), and a lack of confidence in one's abilities.

- **Personalized Assessment:** It's important to conduct a personalized assessment of triggers. What causes anxiety for one person may not be the same for another. Self-awareness and introspection are key in this process.

- **Journaling**: Keeping a journal can help individuals track and identify their anxiety triggers over time. Writing down thoughts, feelings, and situations associated with anxiety can reveal patterns and insights.

Goal Setting:

- **Setting SMART Goals:** Goal setting is a powerful tool for managing performance anxiety. SMART goals are Specific, Measurable, Achievable, Relevant, and Time-bound. These goals provide a clear direction and help individuals focus their efforts.

- **Process vs. Outcome Goals:** Encourage individuals to set both process and outcome goals. Process goals are about the actions and strategies one will employ to perform well, while outcome goals focus on the desired result.

- **Breaking Goals Down:** Large goals can be overwhelming and contribute to anxiety. Break down larger goals into smaller, manageable steps. Achieving these smaller steps can boost confidence.

- **Tracking Progress:** Regularly track progress toward goals. Celebrate successes, and if necessary, adjust goals as circumstances change.

Mindful Performance:

- **Practicing Mindfulness:** Mindfulness involves being fully present in the moment without judgment. Encourage individuals to incorporate mindfulness techniques into their performance preparation and execution.

- **Mindful Breathing:** Deep breathing exercises can be particularly useful before and during performance. Inhaling slowly through the nose and exhaling through the mouth can help calm the nervous system.

- **Visualization:** Visualization is a form of mindfulness where individuals vividly imagine themselves performing successfully. It can reduce anxiety and enhance self-confidence.

- **Staying Present:** Remind individuals to focus on the task at hand rather than worrying about past mistakes or future outcomes. Staying present can help manage anxiety.

Building Resilience:

- **Resilience as a Skill:** Resilience is the ability to bounce back from setbacks and adapt to challenges. It's a skill that can be developed over time.

- **Positive Self-Talk:** Encourage individuals to cultivate a positive and growth-oriented mindset. Self-talk plays a significant role in resilience. When faced with difficulties, individuals with resilience tend to view challenges as opportunities for growth.

- **Emotional Regulation:** Building emotional regulation skills can enhance resilience. Teach strategies like deep breathing, journaling, or seeking social support to manage emotions effectively.

- **Seeking Support:** Resilience is often built with the support of others. Encourage individuals to reach out to friends, family, or mental health professionals for support when needed.

By identifying anxiety triggers, setting SMART goals, practicing mindfulness techniques, and building resilience, individuals can effectively manage and reduce performance anxiety. These strategies empower individuals to perform at their best while facing challenges with confidence and composure.

Chapter 17: Coping with Uncertainty and Change

Change and uncertainty are inherent parts of life. This chapter explores ways to cope with uncertainty, navigate transitions, prepare for college and beyond, and embrace change as an opportunity for personal growth.

Section 1: Navigating Transitions

Transitions can be challenging, whether it's moving to a new school, transitioning to high school, or adjusting to a major life change. In this section, we discuss strategies for navigating transitions:

- **Understanding the Impact of Transitions**: Explore how transitions can evoke anxiety, stress, and fear of the unknown.
- **Developing Adaptability**: Learn how to cultivate adaptability and resilience as essential skills for successfully navigating transitions.
- **Seeking Support**: Understand the importance of seeking support from trusted adults, mentors, or counselors during times of transition.
- **Goal Setting and Planning**: Explore how setting goals and creating plans can provide structure and purpose during transitional periods.

Understanding the Impact of Transitions:

Definition: *Transitions refer to significant life changes or shifts in circumstances. These can include changes in schools, moving to a new city, starting college, or entering the workforce. It's essential to understand that transitions are a normal part of life, but they can also bring uncertainty and stress.*

- **Emotional Responses**: Transitions often elicit a range of emotional responses, including anxiety, fear, excitement, and sadness. Understanding these emotions and their potential impact on mental well-being is crucial.

- **Common Challenges**: Different life transitions come with various challenges. For example, transitioning from high school to college may involve adapting to a new academic environment, while transitioning from college to the workforce may involve navigating the job market and financial independence.

- **Resilience:** Recognize that individuals can develop resilience by effectively coping with transitions. This resilience can help them navigate future changes more confidently.

Developing Adaptability:

- **Adaptability as a Skill:** Adaptability is the ability to adjust to new conditions and effectively manage change. It is a skill that can be developed and honed over time.

- **Flexibility:** Encourage individuals to embrace flexibility and open-mindedness. Being open to new experiences and ways of thinking can make transitions smoother.

- **Problem-Solving:** Developing problem-solving skills is essential in adapting to new situations. Encourage individuals to approach challenges as opportunities to learn and grow.

- **Learning from Change:** Help individuals see change as a chance to learn more about themselves, their strengths, and their values. Change can provide valuable insights into personal growth.

Seeking Support:

- **Social Support:** Encourage individuals to seek support from friends, family, or peers during times of transition. Sharing thoughts and feelings with trusted individuals can provide emotional validation and practical advice.

- **Mental Health Professionals:** If the transition is particularly challenging or accompanied by mental health concerns, seeking support from mental health professionals, such as therapists or counselors, can be invaluable.

- **Support Groups:** Support groups or communities of individuals going through similar transitions can offer a sense of belonging and shared experiences.

- **Building a Support Network:** Actively work on building a support network before and during transitions. Having a reliable support system can reduce the feeling of isolation and increase resilience.

Goal Setting and Planning:

1. **Setting Clear Goals:** During transitions, setting clear, specific goals can provide a sense of purpose and direction. Goals can be related to academics, career, personal development, or lifestyle changes.

2. **Creating a Plan:** Develop a plan for achieving these goals. This plan may include specific actions, timelines, and resources needed.

3. **Flexibility in Goals**: While setting goals is important, individuals should also be open to adjusting their goals as circumstances change. Flexibility in goal setting allows for adaptation to unexpected challenges.

   Importance of Flexibility in Goals:

   1. Adaptation to Changing Circumstances: Life is inherently unpredictable. Unexpected events, both positive and negative, can occur at any time. Flexibility in goal setting allows individuals to respond to these changes by adjusting their objectives as needed. This adaptability is especially crucial during times of transition or uncertainty.

   2. Reduced Stress and Anxiety: When individuals rigidly stick to predefined goals despite changing circumstances, it can lead to frustration, stress, and anxiety. Flexibility in goal setting reduces the pressure to achieve specific outcomes and promotes a more relaxed and adaptive mindset.

   3. Enhanced Resilience: Being open to modifying goals in response to challenges fosters resilience. Resilient individuals view setbacks as opportunities for growth and learning rather than insurmountable obstacles. Flexibility

in goal setting aligns with this resilient mindset.

4. Improved Decision-Making: When individuals assess their goals in light of new information or changing circumstances, they can make more informed and rational decisions. This can lead to better outcomes and a greater sense of control over one's life.

How to Apply Flexibility in Goal Setting:

1. Regular Review: Encourage individuals to periodically review their goals. This review process allows them to assess whether their objectives remain relevant and achievable in light of changing circumstances.
2. Adjusting Priorities: Sometimes, achieving certain goals may require significant sacrifices or effort that individuals are not willing or able to make. Flexibility in goal setting permits them to reprioritize and focus on what matters most at any given time.

3. Setting Milestones: Break down larger goals into smaller, more manageable milestones. This approach allows individuals to track progress and make adjustments as they achieve or encounter challenges in reaching these milestones.

4. Seeking Feedback: Don't hesitate to seek feedback from trusted friends, mentors, or professionals. They can provide valuable insights and alternative perspectives that may lead to goal adjustments.

5. Mindfulness Practice: Incorporating mindfulness techniques can help individuals stay grounded and make decisions in alignment with their values and well-being rather than reacting impulsively to external pressures.

6. Balancing Long-Term and Short-Term Goals: Striking a balance between long-term aspirations and short-term needs is essential. Flexibility in goal setting can involve shifting the focus between these two categories as circumstances evolve.

7. Embracing Growth: Encourage individuals to view goal adjustments as opportunities for personal growth and development. Challenges and setbacks can provide valuable lessons that contribute to resilience and wisdom.

In summary, flexibility in goal setting is an adaptive and essential skill in today's dynamic world. It allows individuals to respond effectively to changing circumstances, reduce stress, and maintain a positive outlook on their life journey. By embracing the fluidity of goals, individuals can achieve a greater sense of control and satisfaction in their lives.

4. **Monitoring Progress:** Regularly monitor progress toward goals and celebrate achievements along the way. This helps maintain motivation and a positive outlook.

Coping with uncertainty and change involves recognizing the impact of transitions, developing adaptability as a skill, seeking support from social networks and professionals, and setting clear goals and plans. With these strategies, individuals can navigate transitions with resilience and confidence, ultimately embracing change as an opportunity for personal growth.

Section 2: Preparing for College and Beyond

Preparing for college and the future can be both exciting and anxiety-inducing. This section offers guidance on preparing for the transition to college and beyond:

- **College Readiness**: Explore steps to prepare for college, including researching colleges, applying for scholarships, and adapting to a new academic environment.
- **Career Planning**: Understand the benefits of career planning, including self-assessment, exploring career options, and setting educational and vocational goals.
- **Balancing Aspirations**: Learn how to balance personal aspirations with realistic expectations, taking into account individual strengths and passions.

- **Resilience in the Face of Uncertainty**: Discover strategies for maintaining resilience and a growth mindset when facing uncertainties about the future.

College Readiness:

- **Academic Preparedness:** College readiness involves ensuring that high school students are academically prepared for the demands of college-level coursework. This includes taking rigorous courses, maintaining a strong GPA, and achieving competitive standardized test scores (SAT or ACT).

- **College Application Process:** Preparing for college also includes understanding and navigating the college application process. This involves researching colleges, writing compelling personal statements, gathering recommendation letters, and meeting application deadlines.

- **Financial Preparedness**: College readiness extends to financial planning. This includes exploring financial aid options, scholarships, and creating a budget for college expenses.

- **Emotional Readiness:** Preparing emotionally for college involves managing expectations and understanding the potential challenges of leaving home, adjusting to a new environment, and building a support network.

Career Planning:

- **Self-Assessment:** Career planning begins with self-assessment. Individuals should reflect on their interests, strengths, values, and long-term goals. This self-awareness forms the foundation for making informed career decisions.

- **Exploration:** Encourage exploration of different career paths through internships, part-time jobs, informational interviews, and job shadowing. Gaining real-world experience helps individuals understand the demands and rewards of various professions.

- **Educational Path:** Depending on their chosen career, individuals may need to plan their educational path, which could involve obtaining specific degrees or certifications.

- **Setting Career Goals:** Career planning involves setting both short-term and long-term career goals. These goals serve as guideposts for making decisions about education, training, and job opportunities.

Balancing Aspirations:

- **Balancing Academic and Extracurricular Activities:** Striking a balance between academic responsibilities and extracurricular interests is crucial. While academic achievement is essential for college admission, participation in extracurricular activities demonstrates a well-rounded individual.

- **Managing Expectations:** Balancing aspirations also involves managing expectations, both one's own and those of parents or guardians. It's essential to recognize that success can take different forms and that there may be multiple pathways to achieving one's goals.

- **Prioritizing Mental Health:** Maintaining balance also includes prioritizing mental health. Overcommitting to academic or extracurricular activities can lead to burnout and stress. Encourage individuals to practice self-care and seek support when needed.

- **Goal Alignment:** Align aspirations with personal values and passions. Pursuing a career or educational path that aligns with one's intrinsic motivations often leads to greater satisfaction and success.

Resilience in the Face of Uncertainty:

- **Coping with Change:** Encourage the development of resilience skills to cope with the uncertainty of college and career choices. Resilience involves adaptability, problem-solving, and the ability to bounce back from setbacks.

- **Acceptance of Uncertainty:** Teach individuals that uncertainty is a natural part of life. Learning to accept and embrace the unknown can reduce anxiety and promote a sense of adventure in pursuing goals.

- **Failure as a Learning Opportunity:** Emphasize that failures and setbacks are not the end but opportunities for growth and learning. Resilient individuals view challenges as stepping stones toward success.

- **Building a Support System:** Developing resilience often involves building a strong support system of friends, mentors, and mental health professionals who can provide guidance and emotional support during challenging times.

Preparing for college, career planning, balancing aspirations, and developing resilience are interconnected processes that require self-awareness, adaptability, and a growth mindset. Encourage individuals to approach these endeavors with curiosity and a willingness to learn, adapt, and grow.

Section 3: Embracing Change as Growth

Change, though challenging, can also lead to personal growth and development. This section focuses on embracing change as an opportunity for positive transformation:

- **Shifting Perspectives**: Explore how changing one's perspective on change can lead to greater acceptance and even excitement about new opportunities.
- **Learning from Change**: Understand how change can be a powerful teacher, providing valuable life experiences and lessons.
- **Building Resilience**: Learn how to build resilience as a tool for effectively navigating change and maintaining emotional well-being.
- **Mindful Adaptation**: Discover the role of mindfulness in adapting to change, reducing anxiety, and staying grounded in the present moment.

Shifting Perspectives:

- **Embracing New Viewpoints:** Shifting perspectives involves the willingness to see situations, challenges, and opportunities from different angles. Encourage individuals to approach change with an open mind and consider alternative viewpoints.

- **Challenging Assumptions:** Often, our perceptions are influenced by assumptions and preconceived notions. Shifting perspectives means questioning these assumptions and being open to the possibility that they may not always hold true.

- **Cultivating Empathy:** Developing empathy for others' perspectives can be a powerful way to shift one's own viewpoint. Encourage individuals to actively listen to others and consider how their experiences and perspectives might differ.

- **Reframing Challenges:** Shifting perspectives can also involve reframing challenges as opportunities for growth and learning. Instead of viewing change as a threat, individuals can see it as a chance to develop new skills and resilience.

Learning from Change:

- **Adapting to New Information**: Change often brings new information and experiences. Learning from change means being receptive to this new knowledge and integrating it into one's understanding of the world.

- **Gaining Resilience:** Change can be a testing ground for resilience. Encourage individuals to reflect on how they've navigated previous changes and what they've learned from those experiences. This reflection can enhance resilience.

- **Skill Development:** Change often requires the development of new skills or the refinement of existing ones. Learning from change means recognizing the skills that have been honed during challenging times.

    - Skill Development in the Face of Change:

        - Change often demands that individuals acquire new skills or enhance existing ones to effectively navigate new circumstances or challenges. Learning from change encompasses recognizing and valuing the skills that naturally develop during these transitions. Here's a more detailed exploration of this process:

1. Adaptation Skills: One of the primary skills developed during change is adaptability. Change can force individuals to adapt to different environments, expectations, or roles. This adaptability involves flexibility, problem-solving, and a willingness to embrace novelty.

2. Resilience: Coping with change inherently builds resilience. Resilience is the capacity to bounce back from setbacks and adversity. Individuals learn to persevere, stay focused on their goals, and maintain a positive outlook even in the face of uncertainty.

3. Communication Skills: Change often requires individuals to communicate effectively with others, whether it's in the context of a new job, a transition to a different phase of life, or adapting to a new social environment. Learning to express thoughts and needs clearly becomes crucial.

4. Time Management: Managing time efficiently is a skill that individuals often develop during transitions. Balancing new responsibilities, setting priorities, and meeting deadlines become essential skills in adapting to change.

5. Problem-Solving: Change often presents unexpected challenges. Individuals learn to analyze problems, devise strategies, and make decisions under pressure. Problem-solving skills are honed as individuals navigate unfamiliar territory.

6. Emotional Intelligence: Change can evoke a wide range of emotions, including stress, anxiety, excitement, and even fear. Learning to understand and manage these emotions effectively is a valuable skill that fosters emotional intelligence.

7. Tech and Digital Literacy: In an increasingly digital world, change often involves adapting to new technologies and digital tools. Individuals may need to become more tech-savvy, enhancing their digital literacy skills.

8. Leadership and Teamwork: Some changes may require individuals to assume leadership roles or work closely with others in a team. Skills related to leadership, collaboration, and conflict resolution are developed in such contexts.

9. Financial Literacy: Major life changes, such as starting college or a new job, may necessitate financial management skills. Individuals learn budgeting, saving, and financial planning to ensure financial stability during transitions.

10. Networking and Relationship-Building: Transition periods often involve building new relationships and expanding one's network. Individuals learn how to establish rapport, network effectively, and maintain valuable connections.

- Recognizing and Valuing These Skills:

  - Learning from change isn't just about acquiring new skills but also recognizing and valuing the skills that naturally emerge during challenging times. It involves:

    1. Self-Reflection: Encourage individuals to reflect on their experiences during times of change. What skills did they develop or refine? How did these skills contribute to their successful adaptation?
    2. Acknowledgment: Recognize and acknowledge personal growth and skill development as a result of change. This validation can boost confidence and motivation for future challenges.
    3. Application: Encourage individuals to apply the skills they've acquired to new situations. The ability to transfer these skills to different contexts is a valuable aspect of learning from change.

  - By recognizing and appreciating the skills cultivated during change, individuals can approach future transitions with greater confidence, knowing that they have a valuable toolkit for navigating life's uncertainties and challenges.

- **Leveraging Change for Growth:** Change can serve as a catalyst for personal growth. Encourage individuals to see change as an opportunity to step out of their comfort zones and expand their horizons.

Building Resilience:

- **Cultivating Adaptability:** Resilience is closely linked to adaptability. It involves the ability to bounce back from adversity and adapt to new circumstances. Building resilience requires practicing adaptability through various life experiences.

- **Positive Mindset:** A resilient mindset focuses on strengths and opportunities rather than dwelling on limitations or failures. Encourage individuals to cultivate a positive and growth-oriented mindset in the face of change.

- **Seeking Support:** Building resilience is not a solitary endeavor. Support from friends, family, mentors, or mental health professionals can be instrumental in developing resilience. Encourage individuals to seek and accept support when needed.

- **Self-Care:** Resilience thrives in a healthy body and mind. Emphasize the importance of self-care practices, such as exercise, mindfulness, and proper nutrition, in building and maintaining resilience.

Mindful Adaptation:

- **Present Moment Awareness:** Mindful adaptation involves being fully present in the moment and acknowledging one's thoughts and emotions without judgment. Mindfulness practices, such as meditation and deep breathing, can foster this awareness.

- **Thoughtful Decision-Making:** Encourage individuals to make decisions thoughtfully and intentionally, considering the potential consequences and aligning choices with their values and goals.

- **Flexibility:** Mindful adaptation is characterized by flexibility. It's the ability to adjust plans and responses as new information or circumstances emerge. Flexibility allows individuals to respond effectively to change.

- **Stress Reduction:** Mindfulness techniques can help reduce stress and anxiety associated with change. By staying grounded in the present moment, individuals can manage their emotional responses more effectively.

Shifting perspectives, learning from change, building resilience, and practicing mindful adaptation are essential skills for navigating life's uncertainties and challenges. Encourage individuals to embrace change as an opportunity for growth and to approach it with curiosity and mindfulness.

By the end of these chapters, readers will have gained insights into managing various forms of anxiety, coping with uncertainty and change, and developing resilience to navigate life's challenges with confidence and optimism.

Chapter 18: Self-Care and Self-Compassion

This chapter focuses on the vital aspects of self-care and self-compassion in managing anxiety effectively.

Section 1: The Importance of Self-Care

Understanding the significance of self-care in nurturing mental and emotional well-being:

- **Defining Self-Care**: Explore what self-care means and why it's crucial for teenagers dealing with anxiety.
- **Physical Self-Care**: Learn about physical self-care practices, including exercise, nutrition, sleep, and relaxation techniques.
- **Emotional Self-Care**: Understand the importance of emotional self-care, such as managing stress, practicing mindfulness, and seeking support.
- **Setting Boundaries**: Discover how setting healthy boundaries in relationships and activities can contribute to self-care.

Defining Self-Care:

- **Holistic Well-Being:** Self-care encompasses a holistic approach to well-being, emphasizing the importance of nurturing one's physical, emotional, and mental health. It involves intentional actions and practices that promote self-preservation and overall health.

- **Individualized Approach**: Self-care is highly individualized. What constitutes self-care for one person may differ from another. It's about understanding one's unique needs, preferences, and limitations and tailoring self-care practices accordingly.

- **Proactive vs. Reactive:** Self-care can be both proactive and reactive. Proactive self-care involves incorporating regular practices into one's routine to maintain well-being, such as exercise, meditation, or journaling. Reactive self-care involves responding to immediate stressors or challenges, like taking a break when feeling overwhelmed.

- **Sustainable and Long-Term:** Effective self-care is sustainable and geared toward long-term health and resilience. It's not just a temporary fix but a commitment to maintaining health and well-being over time.

Physical Self-Care:

- **Nutrition:** Physical self-care begins with nutrition. It involves consuming a balanced diet that provides essential nutrients, vitamins, and minerals. Eating mindfully, staying hydrated, and avoiding excessive processed foods are essential aspects of physical self-care.

- **Exercise:** Regular physical activity is a cornerstone of physical self-care. Exercise not only keeps the body physically fit but also contributes to improved mental health, reduced stress, and enhanced overall well-being.
- **Rest and Sleep:** Adequate rest and quality sleep are crucial for physical and mental recovery. Prioritizing sleep hygiene and creating a sleep-conducive environment is part of self-care.

- **Hygiene and Self-Care Rituals:** Basic hygiene practices, such as bathing, dental care, and skincare, are fundamental components of physical self-care. Engaging in self-care rituals, like a relaxing bath or spa day, can provide additional benefits for physical and emotional well-being.

Emotional Self-Care:

- **Emotion Recognition:** Emotional self-care begins with recognizing and acknowledging one's emotions without judgment. It involves developing emotional intelligence and being in tune with one's feelings.

- **Self-Compassion:** Practicing self-compassion is a vital aspect of emotional self-care. It entails treating oneself with the same kindness and understanding that one would offer to a friend during challenging times.

- **Healthy Outlets:** Emotional self-care involves finding healthy outlets for emotions, such as journaling, art, music, or talking to a trusted friend or therapist. Expressing emotions in constructive ways can prevent emotional suppression.

- **Stress Management:** Managing stress is a key component of emotional self-care. Techniques like mindfulness, deep breathing, and relaxation exercises can help individuals cope with stressors effectively.

Setting Boundaries:

- **Personal Boundaries:** Setting personal boundaries involves defining what is acceptable and unacceptable in terms of treatment, behavior, and expectations from others. It's about recognizing one's limits and communicating them clearly.

- **Time Boundaries:** Time boundaries involve managing one's schedule and allocating time for self-care activities, work, relationships, and personal interests. It's essential for maintaining a healthy work-life balance.

- **Emotional Boundaries:** Emotional boundaries pertain to protecting one's emotional well-being. This may involve limiting exposure to toxic relationships or situations that consistently drain one's emotional resources.

- **Communication:** Effective communication is crucial in setting and maintaining boundaries. It requires assertively expressing one's needs, desires, and limits while respecting the boundaries of others.

Incorporating these elements of self-care into one's daily life can contribute to improved overall well-being, reduced stress, enhanced resilience, and better mental and emotional health. Self-care is not a selfish act but a necessary one for maintaining a balanced and fulfilling life.

Section 2: Practicing Self-Compassion

Self-compassion is a powerful tool for managing anxiety and building resilience:

- **Understanding Self-Compassion**: Define self-compassion and its role in reducing self-criticism and self-judgment.
- **Self-Compassion Techniques**: Explore practical self-compassion techniques, including self-kindness, common humanity, and mindfulness.
- **Cultivating Self-Love**: Learn how to cultivate self-love and acceptance, even in the face of anxiety and imperfections.
- **Resilience and Self-Compassion**: Understand the connection between self-compassion and resilience, and how it can help teenagers bounce back from challenges.

Understanding Self-Compassion:

Definition: *Self-compassion is the practice of treating oneself with the same kindness, care, and understanding that one would offer to a close friend in times of suffering or failure. It involves acknowledging one's own imperfections and challenges without judgment or self-criticism.*

- **Components:** Self-compassion consists of three key components, as defined by Kristin Neff, a pioneer in the field of self-compassion:
    - Self-Kindness: This component involves being gentle and understanding toward oneself, especially when faced with adversity or mistakes. It's about avoiding harsh self-judgment and self-criticism.
    - Common Humanity: Recognizing that suffering and difficulties are a part of the human experience is another aspect of self-compassion. It helps individuals understand that they are not alone in their struggles and that others face similar challenges.
    - Mindfulness: Mindfulness in self-compassion involves holding one's feelings and experiences in balanced awareness. It means acknowledging negative emotions without becoming overwhelmed by them and maintaining a non-judgmental perspective.

- **Benefits**: Self-compassion has been linked to numerous psychological benefits, including reduced anxiety and depression, improved emotional well-being, increased resilience, and better overall mental health. It also fosters a sense of self-worth and helps individuals bounce back from setbacks.

Self-Compassion Techniques:

- **Self-Compassion Meditation:** This guided meditation practice involves directing self-compassionate thoughts and feelings toward oneself. It helps individuals cultivate self-kindness and build a habit of responding to their own suffering with compassion.

- **Positive Self-Talk:** Encouraging positive self-talk is a practical self-compassion technique. It involves countering negative self-critical thoughts with self-affirming and supportive statements.

    - For example, replacing "*I'm a failure*" with "*I made a mistake, and that's okay; everyone makes mistakes.*"

- **Writing Exercises:** Journaling or writing exercises can be effective in promoting self-compassion. Individuals can write compassionate letters to themselves, acknowledging their struggles and offering words of encouragement and understanding.

- **Self-Care Rituals:** Engaging in self-care activities, such as taking time for a soothing bath, practicing yoga, or enjoying a favorite hobby, is a way to express self-compassion. These rituals prioritize one's well-being and can be deeply nurturing.

Cultivating Self-Love:

- **Self-Acceptance:** Cultivating self-love begins with self-acceptance. It involves recognizing and embracing one's strengths, weaknesses, and imperfections. Self-acceptance is the foundation upon which self-love is built.

- **Self-Care:** Engaging in regular self-care practices demonstrates self-love. Taking time to nurture one's physical, emotional, and mental well-being communicates a commitment to self-love.

    - Examples of Self-Care include:
        - Engaging in regular self-care practices is a fundamental expression of self-love. It is a deliberate and conscious commitment to nurturing one's physical, emotional, and mental well-being. Here's a deeper exploration:

- **Physical Self-Care:** This aspect of self-care involves taking steps to maintain and improve one's physical health. It includes activities like regular exercise, a balanced diet, adequate sleep, and hygiene routines. Engaging in physical self-care communicates to oneself that the body is worthy of attention and care.
- **Emotional Self-Care:** Emotional self-care involves acknowledging and tending to one's emotional needs. It includes practices like journaling, talking to a trusted friend or therapist, practicing mindfulness, and engaging in activities that bring joy and emotional fulfillment. This form of self-care is a declaration of self-compassion, showing that one's emotions are valid and deserving of care.
- **Mental Self-Care:** Mental self-care focuses on maintaining cognitive health and mental clarity. It includes activities like reading, learning, meditation, and relaxation techniques. Engaging in mental self-care demonstrates a commitment to nurturing one's intellectual and cognitive well-being.
- **Time Management:** Allocating time for self-care amidst busy schedules is an act of prioritizing oneself. It shows that self-love involves making room for activities that promote overall well-being, even in the midst of life's demands.
- **Stress Reduction:** Self-care often includes practices aimed at reducing stress. Stress management techniques, such as deep breathing exercises or meditation, signify a commitment to emotional and mental equilibrium.
- **Self-Reflection:** Engaging in self-reflection is another form of self-care. It allows individuals to gain insight into their thoughts, emotions, and behaviors, leading to personal growth and self-awareness.

- **Setting Boundaries:** Self-love also involves setting and maintaining healthy boundaries. This means valuing one's own needs and limits and asserting them assertively in relationships and commitments.
  - Examples of Setting Boundaries include:
    - Setting and maintaining healthy boundaries is a crucial component of self-love. It involves valuing one's own

needs, limits, and well-being and asserting them assertively in various aspects of life:

- Respecting Personal Space: Setting boundaries in relationships means respecting one's personal space and autonomy. It communicates that one's physical and emotional boundaries are valid and deserving of respect.
- Protecting Mental Health: Boundaries safeguard mental health by preventing excessive stress, emotional exhaustion, or burnout. For example, setting boundaries at work can help maintain a healthy work-life balance.
- Assertive Communication: Self-love is reflected in assertive communication. It involves expressing one's needs, desires, and limitations clearly and respectfully. This type of communication promotes healthier, more respectful interactions with others.
- Conflict Resolution: Boundaries play a crucial role in conflict resolution. When conflicts arise, individuals who have established clear boundaries are better equipped to negotiate and resolve disagreements while maintaining their self-worth.
- Preventing Resentment: Setting boundaries prevents the buildup of resentment. By communicating needs and limits upfront, individuals can avoid feeling taken advantage of or overwhelmed by others' demands.
- Empowerment: Boundaries empower individuals to make choices that align with their values and well-being. This empowerment is a manifestation of self-love, as it prioritizes one's needs and autonomy.
- In summary, self-care and setting boundaries are essential aspects of self-love. They demonstrate a commitment to one's well-being, physical and emotional health, and personal values. Practicing self-care and setting boundaries can lead to improved relationships, reduced stress, enhanced self-esteem, and a more fulfilling life.

- **Forgiveness:** Forgiving oneself for past mistakes or perceived shortcomings is a powerful act of self-love. It means letting go of self-blame and guilt and recognizing that everyone is fallible.

Resilience and Self-Compassion:

- **Resilience Boost:** Self-compassion plays a vital role in resilience. When individuals practice self-compassion, they are better equipped to cope with adversity and bounce back from setbacks. Self-compassion provides a cushion of self-support during challenging times.

- **Reduced Self-Criticism:** Self-criticism can be a significant obstacle to resilience. Self-compassion counters self-criticism by promoting self-kindness and understanding. This reduces the emotional burden individuals place on themselves during tough situations.

- **Emotional Regulation:** Self-compassion helps individuals regulate their emotions effectively. Instead of becoming overwhelmed by negative emotions, they can approach them with a sense of mindfulness and self-kindness, which can be especially beneficial in times of stress.

- **Improved Problem-Solving:** Self-compassion fosters a healthier perspective on failures or mistakes. Instead of dwelling on self-criticism, individuals are more likely to engage in constructive problem-solving and learn from their experiences, contributing to greater resilience.

Cultivating self-compassion is a transformative journey that enhances well-being, fosters resilience, and promotes a more positive relationship with oneself. It's a valuable skill that can be developed over time through practice and self-awareness.

Section 3: Embracing Imperfection

Embracing imperfection is a key aspect of self-compassion and anxiety management:

- **The Myth of Perfection**: Challenge the myth of perfection and understand how unrealistic expectations can contribute to anxiety.
- **Fostering a Growth Mindset**: Learn how adopting a growth mindset can help teenagers view setbacks as opportunities for growth.
- **Self-Reflection and Acceptance**: Explore the power of self-reflection and self-acceptance in embracing imperfections and building self-esteem.

- **Resilience in Imperfection**: Discover how embracing imperfection fosters resilience and allows teenagers to approach challenges with greater ease.

The Myth of Perfection:

- **Unattainable Standards:** The myth of perfection involves the belief that one must achieve flawless performance or appearance in all areas of life. This unattainable standard can lead to chronic stress, anxiety, and feelings of inadequacy because it sets individuals up for constant self-criticism and dissatisfaction.

- **Negative Consequences:** The pursuit of perfection can have negative consequences on mental and emotional well-being. It often leads to a fear of failure, procrastination, and perfectionistic tendencies, where individuals become overly critical of their own work, leading to paralysis or burnout.

- **Shifting Perspectives:** Recognizing the myth of perfection is a crucial step toward self-compassion. It involves shifting one's perspective from a rigid pursuit of flawlessness to a more balanced view of excellence, where mistakes and imperfections are seen as opportunities for growth and learning.

Fostering a Growth Mindset:

- **Embracing Challenges:** A growth mindset is the belief that abilities and intelligence can be developed through effort and learning. Cultivating a growth mindset involves embracing challenges and setbacks as opportunities for personal and intellectual growth, rather than as indicators of failure.

- **Learning from Failure:** Individuals with a growth mindset view failure as a stepping stone to success. They understand that making mistakes is a natural part of the learning process. This mindset encourages resilience, perseverance, and a willingness to try again despite setbacks.

- **Effort as a Path to Mastery:** In a growth mindset, effort is seen as a path to mastery. This perspective promotes a love of learning and encourages individuals to invest time and energy into their goals, knowing that improvement is possible with dedication.

- **Overcoming Limiting Beliefs:** Fostering a growth mindset involves challenging and overcoming limiting beliefs, such as "I'm not good enough" or "I'll never succeed." It replaces these beliefs with a more positive and growth-oriented narrative.

Self-Reflection and Acceptance:

- **Self-Reflection:** Self-reflection is a process of introspection and examination of one's thoughts, feelings, and behaviors. It allows individuals to gain insight into their motivations, values, and goals. Self-reflection is a key element in fostering self-awareness and personal growth.

- **Acceptance:** Self-acceptance is the act of embracing oneself fully, including one's strengths, weaknesses, and imperfections. It involves acknowledging that being imperfect is part of being human. Self-acceptance is a foundation of self-compassion and mental well-being.

- **Reducing Self-Criticism:** Self-reflection and acceptance work together to reduce self-criticism. Through self-reflection, individuals can identify patterns of negative self-talk and replace them with more compassionate and constructive self-talk.

- **Forgiveness:** Self-reflection and acceptance often lead to self-forgiveness. Forgiving oneself for past mistakes or perceived shortcomings is a powerful act of self-compassion and a step toward emotional healing.

Resilience in Imperfection:

- **Building Resilience:** Resilience involves the ability to bounce back from adversity and setbacks. Embracing imperfection contributes to resilience by teaching individuals that they can adapt and thrive despite their flaws or mistakes.

- **Problem-Solving Skills:** Imperfections often require creative problem-solving. When faced with challenges, individuals learn to find innovative solutions and develop problem-solving skills that enhance resilience.

- **Emotional Regulation:** Resilience in imperfection also relates to emotional regulation. Individuals who accept their imperfections are less likely to be overwhelmed by negative emotions when they encounter difficulties. This emotional balance supports resilience.

- **Adaptation and Growth:** Embracing imperfection leads to a mindset of adaptability and growth. Individuals understand that they can learn from their mistakes and become more resilient by using those experiences as stepping stones to personal development.

In summary, recognizing the myth of perfection, fostering a growth mindset, engaging in self-reflection and acceptance, and embracing imperfection are vital components of self-compassion and personal growth. These practices contribute to improved mental and emotional well-being, enhanced resilience, and a more balanced and compassionate relationship with oneself.

Chapter 19: Parenting a Teen with Anxiety

This chapter provides guidance for parents on supporting their anxious teenagers effectively.

Section 1: How to Approach Your Anxious Teen

Effective approaches for parents in addressing anxiety in their teenagers:

- **Recognizing Signs of Anxiety**: Understand the signs and symptoms of anxiety in teenagers and how they may manifest.
- **Creating a Safe Space**: Learn how to create an open and non-judgmental environment where teenagers feel comfortable discussing their anxiety.
- **Active Listening**: Explore active listening techniques to better understand your teen's perspective and emotions.
- **Offering Reassurance**: Understand the role of reassurance and validation in helping anxious teens feel understood and supported.

Recognizing Signs of Anxiety:

- **Behavioral Changes:** Recognizing signs of anxiety involves observing changes in an individual's behavior. This might include increased restlessness, avoidance of certain situations, or frequent expressions of worry or fear. Behavioral changes can manifest differently in each person, so it's essential to be attentive to shifts from their typical patterns.

- **Physical Symptoms:** Anxiety often presents with physical symptoms such as rapid heartbeat, trembling, sweating, muscle tension, or gastrointestinal discomfort. These physical signs can be indicators of underlying anxiety.

- **Emotional Expressions:** Paying attention to emotional expressions is crucial. Anxiety can manifest as irritability, mood swings, excessive fear, or tearfulness. Individuals may also express their anxiety through verbal cues, such as describing persistent worry or feelings of dread.

- **Social Withdrawal**: Anxiety can lead to social withdrawal or isolation. If someone who was previously outgoing or sociable begins to avoid social gatherings or interactions, it may be a sign of anxiety.

Creating a Safe Space:

- **Non-Judgmental Environment:** Creating a safe space involves offering a non-judgmental and accepting environment where individuals feel comfortable expressing their thoughts and feelings without fear of criticism or ridicule. This safe space encourages open communication.

- **Empathy and Understanding:** Demonstrating empathy and understanding is vital. It means actively trying to see the situation from the individual's perspective, acknowledging their emotions, and validating their feelings, even if you don't fully understand or share their experiences.

- **Privacy and Confidentiality:** Privacy and confidentiality are essential components of a safe space. Individuals need to trust that their disclosures will be kept confidential unless there is an immediate risk to their safety or the safety of others.

- **Comfort and Calmness:** Creating a physically comfortable and calm environment can help individuals feel at ease. This may involve offering a comfortable seating arrangement, ensuring a quiet atmosphere, or providing soothing elements like soft lighting or calming music.

Active Listening:

- **Focus and Presence:** Active listening requires full attention and presence. It involves giving the individual your undivided focus, maintaining eye contact, and eliminating distractions. Show that you are genuinely interested in what they have to say.

- **Reflective Responses:** Active listening often includes reflective responses. This means paraphrasing or summarizing what the individual has shared to ensure you've understood correctly. Reflective responses also involve asking open-ended questions to encourage further discussion.

- **Empathetic Responses:** Responding with empathy is a crucial aspect of active listening. Empathetic responses convey that you understand and share in the individual's emotions, which can help them feel heard and supported.

- **Non-Verbal Cues:** Non-verbal cues, such as nodding in agreement or mirroring the individual's body language, can communicate attentiveness and understanding. Non-verbal cues are essential for reinforcing your active listening.

Offering Reassurance:

- **Validation:** Reassurance often involves validating the individual's feelings and experiences. Acknowledge their emotions as valid and assure them that it's okay to feel the way they do. For example, saying, "It's normal to feel anxious sometimes; many people do" can be reassuring.

- **Problem-Solving Support:** Depending on the situation, offering reassurance can also include problem-solving support. If the individual is open to it, you can discuss potential strategies or resources that may help alleviate their anxiety.

- **Availability:** Let the individual know that you are available to listen and offer support whenever they need it. Reiterate your willingness to help and be there for them, whether it's through conversations, seeking professional help, or simply providing a comforting presence.

- **Avoid Minimizing:** While offering reassurance, it's important to avoid minimizing the individual's concerns. Instead of saying, "Don't worry; it's not a big deal," you can say, "I understand this is challenging for you, and I'm here to support you through it."

Creating a safe space, actively listening, recognizing signs of anxiety, and offering reassurance can be invaluable when helping someone navigate their anxiety. These practices foster trust, communication, and emotional support, which can make a significant difference in an individual's well-being and their ability to cope with anxiety.

Section 2: Communication Strategies

Communication strategies that promote constructive dialogue and connection:

- **Effective Communication**: Learn effective communication strategies, including the use of "I" statements, active questioning, and reflective listening.
- **Empathy and Understanding**: Understand the importance of empathy and validating your teen's feelings, even when you may not fully comprehend their anxiety.
- **Managing Conflict**: Discover conflict resolution techniques that help parents and teenagers navigate disagreements related to anxiety.
- **Collaborative Decision-Making**: Explore the benefits of involving your teen in decision-making processes related to their anxiety treatment and management.

Effective Communication:

- **Clarity and Transparency:** Effective communication involves being clear and transparent in your messages. It means expressing your thoughts, feelings, and expectations in a straightforward manner, avoiding ambiguity or vague language.

- **Active Listening:** Active listening is a crucial component of effective communication. It involves fully concentrating on what the other person is saying, asking clarifying questions, and providing feedback to ensure that you've understood their message accurately.

- **Non-Verbal Communication:** Non-verbal cues, such as body language and facial expressions, play a significant role in effective communication. These cues can convey emotions and intentions that may not be expressed verbally. Being mindful of non-verbal communication enhances understanding.

- **Respect for Diverse Perspectives:** Effective communication respects diverse perspectives and viewpoints. It involves acknowledging that different people may have unique opinions and experiences and valuing those differences.

Empathy and Understanding:

- **Empathetic Listening:** Empathy is the ability to understand and share in someone else's feelings. Empathetic listening means not only hearing what the other person is saying but also trying to grasp their emotional experience. It involves acknowledging their emotions and expressing support.

- **Perspective-Taking:** Empathy goes beyond sympathy; it involves perspective-taking. It means attempting to see the situation from the other person's point of view, which can lead to a deeper understanding of their feelings and needs.

- **Validation:** Empathy often includes validation, where you acknowledge the other person's emotions as valid and worthy of recognition. Validating someone's feelings can provide comfort and reassurance.

- **Cultural Sensitivity:** Being empathetic and understanding also involves cultural sensitivity. Recognize that individuals from different cultural backgrounds may have unique norms, values, and communication styles. Respect for cultural diversity enhances empathy.

Managing Conflict:

- **Open and Constructive Communication:** Conflict is a natural part of human interactions. Managing conflict effectively entails engaging in open and constructive communication rather than avoiding or escalating issues. It means addressing concerns and differences in a respectful and solution-oriented manner.

- **Active Problem-Solving:** Conflict management often involves active problem-solving. This includes identifying the root causes of the conflict, brainstorming solutions, and collaborating on mutually agreeable resolutions.

- **Emotional Regulation:** Managing conflict requires emotional regulation. It involves staying calm and composed during difficult conversations, avoiding escalations, and focusing on the issues at hand rather than personal attacks.

- **Seeking Common Ground:** Effective conflict management aims to find common ground and shared interests. It involves searching for solutions that can satisfy both parties' needs and concerns.

Collaborative Decision-Making:

- **Shared Decision-Making:** Collaborative decision-making is a process where individuals work together to make choices that impact them both. It values the input and perspectives of all involved parties, fostering a sense of ownership and commitment to the decisions made.

- **Information Sharing:** In collaborative decision-making, there is an emphasis on sharing relevant information transparently. This allows all parties to make informed choices and contribute meaningfully to the decision-making process.

- **Consensus Building:** Collaborative decision-making aims to reach consensus when possible. This means finding solutions that everyone can support, even if compromises are necessary. Consensus building fosters cooperation and minimizes conflict.

- **Respect for Autonomy:** While collaborative, this approach also respects individual autonomy. It recognizes that individuals have the right to make choices that align with their values and preferences, and decisions should not be imposed.

In summary, effective communication, empathy and understanding, managing conflict, and collaborative decision-making are essential skills for building healthy relationships and resolving interpersonal issues. These practices promote mutual respect, trust, and cooperation, leading to more harmonious and productive interactions with others.

Section 3: Avoiding Common Pitfalls

Common pitfalls to avoid when parenting an anxious teenager:

- **Overprotection**: Understand the potential consequences of overprotecting your teenager and how it can hinder their development.

- **Invalidating Experiences**: Learn to avoid invalidating your teen's experiences or dismissing their anxiety as trivial.
- **Comparisons and Expectations**: Recognize the harm of comparing your teenager to others or setting unrealistic expectations.
- **Seeking Professional Help**: Understand when and how to seek professional help for your anxious teen and the importance of early intervention.

Overprotection:

- **Excessive Control:** Overprotection involves an excessive need to control or shield someone from perceived harm or difficulty. This often arises from a well-intentioned desire to keep loved ones safe. However, it can lead to negative consequences, including limiting the individual's autonomy and decision-making abilities.

- **Impact on Autonomy:** Overprotection can hinder the development of independence and decision-making skills. When individuals are constantly shielded from challenges or decisions, they may struggle to develop the confidence and resilience needed to navigate life's difficulties.

- **Striking a Balance:** Recognizing the need to strike a balance between protection and autonomy is essential. Encouraging individuals to take calculated risks, make choices, and learn from their experiences helps build self-confidence and prepares them for future challenges.

Invalidating Experiences:

- **Emotional Validity:** Invalidation occurs when someone dismisses or minimizes another person's emotional experiences or feelings. It can be detrimental because it invalidates the individual's emotions, making them feel unheard and unsupported.

- **Impact on Mental Health:** Repeated invalidation can contribute to feelings of self-doubt and low self-esteem. It may also discourage individuals from expressing their emotions, leading to emotional suppression and potential mental health issues.

- **Active Listening and Validation**: To combat invalidation, it's important to practice active listening and validation. This involves empathetic listening and acknowledging the individual's feelings as valid, even if you don't fully understand or agree with them. It helps individuals feel heard and supported.

Comparisons and Expectations:

- **Comparisons to Others:** Making constant comparisons between individuals and others can lead to feelings of inadequacy. It fosters a competitive mindset rather than one of self-improvement and self-acceptance.

- **Setting Unrealistic Expectations:** Unrealistic expectations can create significant pressure and stress. When individuals are constantly striving to meet high standards, they may experience anxiety, burnout, or a sense of failure when they inevitably fall short.

- **Encouraging Individual Growth:** Instead of comparing individuals to others or setting unrealistic expectations, it's beneficial to encourage personal growth and self-acceptance. Emphasize that it's okay to have unique strengths and weaknesses, and that progress and self-improvement should be the focus, not perfection.

Seeking Professional Help:

- **Recognizing When Help is Needed:** Seeking professional help is a vital step when individuals are facing challenges beyond their capacity to manage independently. This includes issues related to mental health, emotional well-being, addiction, or significant life changes.

- **Reducing Stigma:** Encouraging the seeking of professional help can help reduce the stigma surrounding mental health issues. It communicates that reaching out for support is a sign of strength, not weakness.

- **Access to Expertise:** Professionals, such as therapists, counselors, or medical practitioners, have specialized expertise and tools to address various mental health and emotional challenges. They can provide guidance, therapy, and interventions tailored to individual needs.

- **Early Intervention:** Seeking professional help early can prevent issues from worsening and promote faster recovery. It's important to emphasize the value of early intervention and not waiting until problems become unmanageable.

In summary, addressing overprotection, invalidating experiences, the harmful effects of comparisons and unrealistic expectations, and the importance of seeking professional help are essential for promoting healthy relationships, self-acceptance, and emotional well-being. These practices encourage autonomy, validation, and a supportive environment for individuals to thrive and overcome challenges.

Chapter 20: Moving Forward

The final chapter emphasizes celebrating progress, setting future goals, and acknowledging the ongoing journey of anxiety recovery.

Section 1: Celebrating Progress

The importance of recognizing and celebrating achievements and milestones:

- **Acknowledging Growth**: Understand the significance of acknowledging and celebrating the progress made in managing anxiety.
- **Small Wins**: Learn how to appreciate small victories and the positive steps taken towards anxiety management.
- **Building Confidence**: Discover how celebrating progress builds confidence and motivates further efforts.
- **Gratitude Practice**: Explore the benefits of incorporating gratitude into daily life as a way to appreciate achievements and blessings.

Acknowledging Growth:

- **Self-Reflection:** Acknowledging growth begins with self-reflection. Encourage individuals to take moments to assess their progress, accomplishments, and personal development. This can include recognizing how they've changed, overcome challenges, or acquired new skills and knowledge.

- **Setting Milestones:** Setting specific milestones or markers of progress can help individuals track their growth. Whether in personal relationships, academics, or other aspects of life, establishing clear goals and measuring their achievement provides a tangible way to acknowledge growth.

- **Expressing Self-Appreciation:** Self-appreciation involves recognizing and appreciating one's efforts and achievements. This can be as simple as saying to oneself, "I've come a long way," or "I'm proud of what I've accomplished." Self-affirmation reinforces positive self-perception.

Small Wins:

- **Breaking Down Goals:** Celebrating small wins entails breaking down larger goals into manageable, bite-sized tasks or milestones. When individuals achieve these smaller objectives, it provides a sense of accomplishment and motivation to keep progressing.

- **Boosting Motivation:** Acknowledging and celebrating small wins is an effective way to boost motivation. It provides a sense of immediate gratification and reinforces the idea that progress is being made, even if the ultimate goal is still ahead.

- **Fostering a Growth Mindset:** Recognizing small wins fosters a growth mindset, where individuals believe in their ability to develop skills and capabilities over time. It encourages them to view challenges as opportunities for growth rather than as insurmountable obstacles.

Building Confidence:

- **Positive Self-Talk:** Building confidence often begins with positive self-talk. Encourage individuals to challenge self-doubt and negative self-perceptions by replacing them with positive affirmations and thoughts. This helps individuals develop a more optimistic self-view.

- **Competence and Mastery:** Confidence is built through competence and mastery. Encourage individuals to set achievable goals that allow them to develop and demonstrate their skills and abilities. Each accomplishment contributes to increased self-assurance.

- **Accepting Imperfection:** Building confidence also involves accepting imperfection. Remind individuals that nobody is perfect, and mistakes are part of the learning process. Learning from failures and setbacks contributes to personal growth and resilience.

Gratitude Practice:

- **Daily Reflection**: A gratitude practice involves daily reflection on things individuals are grateful for. This can include simple pleasures, moments of kindness, or positive experiences. Encourage individuals to keep a gratitude journal where they write down these reflections.

- **Positive Outlook:** Practicing gratitude promotes a more positive outlook on life. It shifts the focus from what's lacking or negative to what's abundant and positive. This change in perspective can significantly impact overall well-being and mental health.

- **Enhancing Resilience:** Gratitude is linked to enhanced resilience. It can help individuals cope with stress and adversity by reminding them of the positive aspects of their lives and providing a buffer against negative emotions.

- **Building Social Connections:** Expressing gratitude often involves acknowledging the kindness of others. This can strengthen social connections and relationships as individuals express their appreciation to those who have supported or helped them.

Incorporating these practices into one's daily life can contribute to personal growth, increased confidence, and a more positive outlook. Acknowledging growth, celebrating small wins, building confidence, and practicing gratitude all foster a sense of empowerment and resilience in the face of life's challenges.

Section 2: Setting Future Goals

The role of setting and working toward future goals in anxiety management:

- **Setting SMART Goals**: Understand the concept of SMART (Specific, Measurable, Achievable, Relevant, Time-bound) goals and how they apply to anxiety management.
- **Long-Term Vision**: Explore the importance of having a long-term vision and purpose in managing anxiety.
- **Personal Growth Goals**: Learn how setting goals for personal growth and resilience contributes to overall well-being.
- **Flexibility and Adaptability**: Understand the value of adapting goals as circumstances change and new challenges arise.

Setting SMART Goals:

- **Specific:** SMART goals are Specific, meaning they are clear, well-defined, and focused. Instead of setting a vague goal like "improve grades," a Specific goal would be "raise my math grade from a B to an A by the end of the semester." Specificity helps individuals clearly understand what they are working toward.

- **Measurable:** Measurable goals are quantifiable and provide a way to track progress. In the example above, "raise my math grade from a B to an A" is measurable because it involves a specific grade improvement that can be measured objectively.

- **Achievable:** Achievable goals are realistic and attainable within the individual's abilities and resources. Setting goals that are too far-fetched or unattainable can lead to frustration and demotivation. SMART goals ensure that objectives are within reach.

- **Relevant:** Relevant goals are aligned with an individual's values, interests, and overall objectives. They should make sense within the context of the individual's life and aspirations. A relevant goal connects with the bigger picture.

- **Time-Bound:** Time-bound goals have a set timeframe for accomplishment. They include a deadline or target date, which creates a sense of urgency and accountability. In our example, the timeframe is "by the end of the semester."

Long-Term Vision:

- **Clarifying Purpose:** Having a long-term vision helps individuals clarify their purpose and direction in life. It provides a sense of meaning and a roadmap for the future. This vision often involves setting big-picture goals and aspirations.

- **Motivation:** A long-term vision serves as a powerful source of motivation. It inspires individuals to take action, make choices, and persevere through challenges because they have a clear sense of what they are working toward.

- **Flexibility:** While a long-term vision provides direction, it should also be flexible enough to adapt to changing circumstances and evolving personal priorities. Life is dynamic, and the ability to adjust one's long-term vision can be a sign of resilience and adaptability.

- **Breaking Down into Short-Term Goals:** To achieve a long-term vision, individuals often break it down into smaller, manageable short-term goals. These short-term goals become stepping stones toward the larger vision, making the path to success more achievable.

Personal Growth Goals:

- **Continuous Improvement:** Personal growth goals are centered around self-improvement and development. These goals can encompass various aspects of life, such as education, skills, relationships, or emotional well-being. The pursuit of personal growth fosters resilience and adaptability.

- **Embracing Challenges:** Personal growth often involves embracing challenges and stepping out of one's comfort zone. It encourages individuals to take on new experiences, learn from failures, and adapt to changing circumstances.

- **Self-Reflection:** Achieving personal growth goals often requires self-reflection and self-awareness. Individuals must assess their strengths, weaknesses, values, and aspirations to set meaningful goals that align with their personal growth journey.

- **Building Resilience:** The pursuit of personal growth inherently builds resilience. It teaches individuals to bounce back from setbacks, overcome obstacles, and adapt to changing circumstances as they work toward becoming the best versions of themselves.

Flexibility and Adaptability:

- **Openness to Change:** Flexibility and adaptability involve being open to change and receptive to new ideas or circumstances. It's about embracing change as a natural part of life rather than resisting it.

- **Problem-Solving Skills:** These traits are closely related to problem-solving skills. When individuals encounter challenges or unexpected changes, they are better equipped to find solutions and navigate through uncertainty.

- **Stress Management:** Flexibility and adaptability also contribute to effective stress management. Resisting change or being inflexible can lead to increased stress, while adaptability allows individuals to cope more effectively with stressors.

- **Embracing Opportunities:** Being flexible and adaptable allows individuals to seize opportunities that may arise unexpectedly. It enables them to adjust their plans and strategies in response to new possibilities.

In summary, setting SMART goals, having a long-term vision, pursuing personal growth goals, and emphasizing flexibility and adaptability are essential aspects of personal development and resilience. These practices help individuals define their path, stay motivated, and navigate life's challenges with resilience and optimism.

Section 3: The Journey of Anxiety Recovery

Reflecting on the ongoing journey of anxiety recovery:

- **The Nonlinear Path**: Recognize that anxiety recovery is a nonlinear journey with ups and downs.
- **Self-compassion in Recovery**: Understand how self-compassion plays a crucial role in navigating setbacks and maintaining progress.
- **Resilience and Adaptation**: Explore how building resilience and adaptability enhances the ability to manage anxiety effectively.
- **Support and Community**: Reflect on the importance of ongoing support, whether from professionals, family, or peer networks, throughout the journey of anxiety recovery.

The Nonlinear Path:

- **Understanding the Journey:** Recovery is rarely a linear process. It's essential to understand that setbacks, relapses, and fluctuations in progress are normal. Instead of viewing these as failures, individuals can see them as opportunities for learning and growth.

- **Learning from Setbacks:** Nonlinear paths in recovery provide opportunities to learn from setbacks. Individuals can identify triggers, coping strategies that may not have been effective, and areas where additional support is needed. This reflective process can lead to stronger resilience.

- **Patience and Persistence:** Navigating a nonlinear path requires patience and persistence. It's important to remind individuals that recovery is an ongoing journey, and setbacks do not erase the progress they've made. Encourage them to continue working toward their goals, even when faced with challenges.

Self-compassion in Recovery:

- **Kindness Toward Oneself:** Self-compassion involves treating oneself with the same kindness and understanding that one would offer to a friend. In recovery, it's crucial to practice self-compassion, especially during difficult times. Instead of self-criticism, individuals can offer themselves words of comfort and encouragement.

- **Reducing Self-Stigma:** Self-compassion can help reduce self-stigma associated with mental health challenges or addiction. When individuals show themselves understanding and kindness, they are less likely to internalize negative societal attitudes.

- **Boosting Resilience:** Self-compassion is closely linked to resilience. It helps individuals bounce back from setbacks by fostering a positive self-view and a sense of self-worth, even in the face of difficulties.

Resilience and Adaptation:

- **Facing Change:** Resilience is the ability to adapt and bounce back from adversity. In recovery, individuals often face significant changes in their lives, such as breaking free from addiction or managing mental health conditions. Resilience allows them to navigate these changes effectively.

- **Learning and Growth:** Resilience involves learning and growth through adversity. When individuals encounter challenges in recovery, they can develop new coping strategies, problem-solving skills, and emotional regulation techniques. This growth contributes to greater resilience.

- **Positive Outlook:** Resilience fosters a positive outlook on the future. It helps individuals believe in their ability to overcome obstacles and adapt to new circumstances, which can be particularly valuable in long-term recovery.

Support and Community:

- **Shared Experiences:** Support and community provide a sense of belonging and shared experiences. Individuals in recovery benefit from connecting with others who have faced similar challenges. This connection reduces feelings of isolation and stigma.

- **Accountability:** Support networks and communities often provide accountability. Knowing that others are cheering for their success motivates individuals to stay on track with their recovery goals.

- **Resources and Guidance:** Communities can offer valuable resources and guidance. This may include access to therapy, peer support groups, educational materials, and practical advice for managing recovery.

- **Inspiration:** Being part of a supportive community can inspire individuals in recovery. Seeing others who have successfully overcome similar challenges can instill hope and determination, reinforcing their own commitment to recovery.

In summary, understanding the nonlinear path of recovery, practicing self-compassion, nurturing resilience and adaptability, and embracing the support of a community are essential components of a successful recovery journey. These aspects provide individuals with the tools, mindset, and connections needed to navigate the challenges of recovery and build a healthier, more resilient life.

By the end of this book, readers will have gained comprehensive insights into self-care, self-compassion, and the management of anxiety. Parents will also have valuable guidance on supporting their anxious teenagers, and everyone will be equipped with strategies for moving forward and continuing the journey of anxiety recovery with confidence and hope.

Conclusion

In this concluding chapter, we reflect on the transformative power of resilience, offer encouragement and hope to teenagers facing anxiety, and share final thoughts on the journey toward well-being.

Section 1: The Power of Resilience

Resilience has been a recurring theme throughout this book, and in this section, we revisit its importance:

- **Recap of Resilience**: Summarize the key concepts and strategies for building resilience discussed throughout the book.
- **Resilience Stories**: Share inspiring stories of teenagers who have overcome anxiety through resilience, highlighting their journeys and achievements.
- **Empowering the Future**: Explore how resilience serves as a lifelong tool for facing challenges and fostering mental and emotional well-being.

Section 2: Encouragement and Hope for Teens

Addressing anxious teenagers directly, this section offers words of encouragement and hope:

- **You Are Not Alone**: Remind teenagers that they are not alone in their struggles with anxiety and that many have overcome similar challenges.
- **The Potential for Change**: Highlight the potential for positive change and personal growth, even in the face of anxiety.
- **Believe in Yourself**: Encourage self-belief and self-compassion as fundamental elements of the journey toward well-being.
- **The Future Awaits**: Emphasize the exciting opportunities and adventures that await teenagers as they continue their journey.

Section 3: Final Thoughts

In this section, we offer some final reflections on the broader message of the book:

- **Anxiety as a Teacher**: Encourage readers to view anxiety not solely as an adversary but as a teacher that can foster resilience and personal growth.
- **The Role of Support**: Highlight the importance of seeking and accepting support, whether from family, friends, professionals, or support networks.
- **The Journey Continues**: Acknowledge that the journey toward well-being is ongoing and that each step, no matter how small, contributes to a brighter future.
- **A Message of Hope**: Conclude with a message of hope, emphasizing that anxiety need not define one's life, and a fulfilling, joyful future is within reach.

Appendices

The appendices provide additional resources, practical tools, and further reading recommendations to support teenagers on their journey to managing anxiety effectively.

Appendix A: Additional Resources for Teens

This section offers a curated list of additional resources, including websites, helplines, and organizations, that provide valuable information and support for teenagers dealing with anxiety.

1. **National Institute of Mental Health (NIMH)**
   Website: https://www.nimh.nih.gov/ NIMH provides extensive information on mental health conditions, treatment options, and research updates. It's a valuable resource for understanding anxiety disorders and other mental health issues.

2. **Anxiety and Depression Association of America (ADAA)**
   Website: https://adaa.org/ ADAA offers resources, articles, and webinars on anxiety and depression. Their "Find a Therapist" tool can help teens locate mental health professionals in their area.

3. **National Alliance on Mental Illness (NAMI)**
   Website: https://www.nami.org/ NAMI provides support, education, and advocacy for individuals and families affected by mental illness. They offer programs and resources specifically designed for young adults.

4. **Crisis Text Line**
   Text "HELLO" to 741741 Crisis Text Line provides free, confidential text-based support for individuals in crisis. Trained crisis counselors are available 24/7 to provide assistance and emotional support.

5. **The Trevor Project**
   Website: https://www.thetrevorproject.org/ The Trevor Project focuses on providing crisis intervention and suicide prevention services for LGBTQ+ youth. They offer a lifeline, chat, and text support.

6. **Teen Mental Health**
   Website: https://teenmentalhealth.org/ Teen Mental Health offers a range of resources, including educational materials and toolkits, to promote mental health awareness and well-being among teenagers.

7. **Mindful Schools**
   Website: https://www.mindfulschools.org/ Mindful Schools offers online mindfulness and meditation courses specifically designed for students. These practices can help reduce stress and improve emotional well-being.

8. **7 Cups**
   Website: https://www.7cups.com/ 7 Cups is an online platform that provides free, anonymous emotional support through chat rooms and one-on-one conversations with trained listeners.

9. **Child Mind Institute**
   Website: https://childmind.org/ The Child Mind Institute offers a wide range of resources and articles on children and teen mental health, including information on anxiety and treatment options.

10. **Local Support Groups**
    Check with local mental health organizations, schools, or community centers for information on local support groups or counseling services available to teens in your area.

Remember that seeking help and support is a sign of strength, and there are many resources available to assist teenagers in managing anxiety and promoting overall mental well-being. Whether through online platforms, hotlines, or local services, these resources can provide valuable assistance on the journey to relief and recovery.

Appendix B: Worksheets and Exercises

Appendix B contains a collection of worksheets and exercises designed to help teenagers apply the strategies and concepts discussed in the book in a practical and interactive way.

Worksheet 1: Anxiety Journal
Instructions: Use this journal to track your anxiety triggers, symptoms, and coping strategies. Record the date and time of each entry.

- Date & Time: _______________________________
- Trigger: _______________________________
- Symptoms: _______________________________
- Coping Strategies: _______________________

Worksheet 2: Mindfulness Meditation Guide

Instructions: Practice mindfulness meditation with this guided exercise. Find a quiet, comfortable space to sit or lie down. Focus on your breath and let go of thoughts as they come.

Close your eyes and take a deep breath in.

Hold your breath for a few seconds.

Exhale slowly, letting go of any tension.

Continue to breathe deeply and naturally.

Pay attention to the sensation of your breath entering and leaving your body.

If your mind wanders, gently bring your focus back to your breath.

Practice for 5-10 minutes daily.

Worksheet 3: Breathing Exercise

Instructions: Use this exercise to practice deep breathing for relaxation. Sit or lie down comfortably.

Inhale slowly through your nose for a count of 4.

Hold your breath for a count of 4.

Exhale slowly through your mouth for a count of 6.

Repeat this cycle for 2-3 minutes.

Worksheet 4: Cognitive Restructuring

Instructions: Identify and challenge negative thought patterns with this exercise.

- Negative Thought: _______________________________
- Evidence Against the Thought: _______________
- Alternative, Balanced Thought: _______________

Worksheet 5: Goal Setting

Instructions: Set SMART goals for managing anxiety.

- Specific: _______________________________
- Measurable: _______________________________
- Achievable: _______________________________
- Relevant: _______________________________

- Time-Bound: _________________________________

Worksheet 6: Gratitude Journal

Instructions: Write down three things you're grateful for each day.

____

____

____

Worksheet 7: Self-Compassion Exercise

Instructions: Practice self-compassion by completing the following sentences:

I am proud of myself for...

Today, I showed kindness to myself when...

I forgive myself for...

I deserve love and happiness because…

Worksheet 8: Resilience-Building Exercise

Instructions: Reflect on your resilience and strengths.

One challenge I've overcome in the past is...

Something I've learned from difficult times is...

A skill or quality that makes me resilient is...

I believe in my ability to handle challenges because...

Feel free to customize these worksheets and exercises to fit the specific needs and preferences of your target audience. Encourage teenagers to complete these exercises regularly as part of their anxiety relief and resilience-building journey.

Appendix C: Recommended Reading List

For those interested in further exploration, this section provides a list of recommended books and resources on anxiety, resilience, and personal development.

For Teens:

1. The Anxiety Survival Guide for Teens: CBT Skills to Overcome Fear, Worry, and Panic by Jennifer Shannon LMFT

2. My Anxious Mind: A Teen's Guide to Managing Anxiety and Panic by Michael A. Tompkins and Katherine A. Martinez
3. Don't Let Your Emotions Run Your Life for Teens: Dialectical Behavior Therapy Skills for Helping You Manage Mood Swings, Control Angry Outbursts, and Get Along with Others by Sheri Van Dijk MSW
4. The Stress Reduction Workbook for Teens: Mindfulness Skills to Help You Deal with Stress by Gina M. Biegel MA LMFT
5. The Gifted Teen Survival Guide: Smart, Sharp, and Ready for (Almost) Anything by Judy Galbraith M.A. and Jim Delisle Ph.D.
6. The Teen Girl's Anxiety Survival Guide: Ten Ways to Conquer Anxiety and Feel Your Best by Lucie Hemmen PhD
7. Mindfulness for Teens with ADHD: A Skill-Building Workbook to Help You Focus and Succeed by Debra Burdick LCSW BCN

For Parents and Caregivers:
1. The Anxiety and Phobia Workbook by Edmund J. Bourne PhD
2. Freeing Your Child from Anxiety: Powerful, Practical Solutions to Overcome Your Child's Fears, Worries, and Phobias by Tamar E. Chansky PhD
3. Helping Your Anxious Teen: Positive Parenting Strategies to Help Your Teen Beat Anxiety, Stress, and Worry by Sheila Achar Josephs PhD
4. The Whole-Brain Child: 12 Revolutionary Strategies to Nurture Your Child's Developing Mind by Daniel J. Siegel MD and Tina Payne Bryson PhD
5. Raising An Emotionally Intelligent Child The Heart of Parenting by John Gottman PhD and Joan Declaire
6. Anxious Kids, Anxious Parents: 7 Ways to Stop the Worry Cycle and Raise Courageous and Independent Children by Reid Wilson PhD and Lynn Lyons LICSW
7. The Resilience Workbook: Essential Skills to Recover from Stress, Trauma, and Adversity by Glenn R. Schiraldi PhD

General Resources:
1. The Relaxation and Stress Reduction Workbook by Martha Davis PhD, Elizabeth Robbins Eshelman MSW, and Matthew McKay PhD
2. The Power of Now: A Guide to Spiritual Enlightenment by Eckhart Tolle
3. Mind Over Mood: Change How You Feel by Changing the Way You Think by Dennis Greenberger PhD and Christine A. Padesky PhD
4. The 7 Habits of Highly Effective Teens by Sean Covey

5. The Anxiety Toolkit: Strategies for Fine-Tuning Your Mind and Moving Past Your Stuck Points by Alice Boyes PhD
6. The Gifts of Imperfection: Let Go of Who You Think You're Supposed to Be and Embrace Who You Are by Brené Brown PhD LMSW
7. Daring Greatly: How the Courage to Be Vulnerable Transforms the Way We Live, Love, Parent, and Lead by Brené Brown PhD LMSW

Please note that book availability may vary based on location and publication date. Encourage teens and their families to explore these resources as part of their journey toward anxiety relief and personal growth.

Appendix D: Glossary of Terms

The glossary of terms provides definitions and explanations of key concepts and terminology related to anxiety, mental health, and well-being, making it a valuable reference for readers seeking clarity on specific terms used in the book.

1. **Anxiety:** A state of uneasiness or apprehension often accompanied by worry, fear, or nervousness.
2. **Anxiety Disorder**: A mental health condition characterized by excessive and persistent anxiety, fear, or worry that can interfere with daily life.
3. **Cognitive Behavioral Therapy (CBT):** A therapeutic approach that helps individuals identify and change negative thought patterns and behaviors contributing to anxiety.
4. **Mindfulness:** The practice of being fully present in the moment, often used to reduce stress and anxiety.
5. **Panic Attack:** A sudden and intense episode of extreme anxiety or fear, often accompanied by physical symptoms such as rapid heartbeat and shortness of breath.
6. **Resilience:** The ability to bounce back and adapt positively to adversity, stress, or challenges.
7. **Self-Compassion:** Treating oneself with kindness, understanding, and forgiveness, especially during difficult times.
8. **Stress:** A physiological and emotional response to perceived threats or demands that can lead to feelings of tension and anxiety.

9. **Therapist:** A trained mental health professional who provides counseling, therapy, and support for individuals dealing with anxiety and other mental health issues.
10. **Triggers:** Specific situations, thoughts, or events that can cause or worsen anxiety symptoms.
11. **Well-Being:** A state of physical, mental, and emotional health and happiness.
12. **Coping Strategies:** Techniques and practices used to manage and reduce anxiety and stress.
13. **Emotional Regulation:** The ability to effectively manage and control one's emotions.
14. **Mindfulness Meditation:** A practice that involves focusing on the present moment and cultivating awareness without judgment.
15. **Social Support:** Emotional, practical, and instrumental assistance from friends, family, or a community that can provide comfort and help in times of need.
16. **Self-Efficacy:** Belief in one's ability to achieve goals and overcome challenges.
17. **Growth Mindset:** The belief that abilities and intelligence can be developed and improved over time through effort and learning.
18. **Exposure Therapy:** A therapeutic technique that involves gradually facing feared situations or triggers to reduce anxiety and phobias.
19. **Goal Setting:** The process of defining specific, measurable, achievable, relevant, and time-bound (SMART) objectives.
20. **Perfectionism:** A tendency to set unrealistically high standards for oneself and strive for flawlessness.

This glossary provides definitions for key terms used throughout the book to help readers better understand the concepts and terminology related to anxiety relief and mental well-being.

Acknowledgments

Writing a book is a journey that often involves the support and encouragement of many individuals. I would like to take this opportunity to express my gratitude to those who have contributed to the creation of this book.

First and foremost, I want to thank the teenagers who have inspired this work. Your resilience, strength, and willingness to confront anxiety head-on are truly remarkable. It is my hope that this book serves as a valuable resource on your path to greater well-being.

To the parents, guardians, and caregivers who play a crucial role in supporting and guiding teenagers through their challenges, thank you for your dedication and love. Your commitment to understanding and helping your teens is commendable.

I extend my appreciation to the mental health professionals, educators, and experts in the field of adolescent anxiety who have shared their knowledge and insights. Your expertise has been invaluable in shaping the content of this book.

I also want to thank my family and friends for their unwavering support and encouragement throughout this writing process. Your belief in the importance of this work has been a constant source of motivation.
Lastly, to the readers of this book, thank you for choosing to embark on this journey toward anxiety relief for teens. It is my sincere hope that the information and strategies presented here prove beneficial in your quest for improved mental well-being.

Remember, you are not alone in this journey, and there is hope and help available. Together, we can work towards a future where anxiety is not an insurmountable obstacle but a challenge that can be overcome.
With gratitude,

Avi Quinn

About the Author

Avi Quinn is not just an author but a dedicated parent, empathetic individual, and someone who has navigated the challenges of anxiety and stress firsthand. With three children of their own, Avi Quinn understands the profound impact that anxiety can have on young lives and the families who support them.

Having personally experienced anxiety and witnessed its effects within their own family, Avi Quinn felt a deep calling to shed light on this often daunting journey. This book is a testament to their unwavering commitment to providing guidance and support to others who may be grappling with anxiety and stress.

Avi Quinn's unique perspective, as both a caring parent and someone who has faced anxiety head-on, has informed the creation of this guidebook. Their heartfelt desire is to ensure that no one feels lost in the darkness of anxiety, and that every teenager and their family can find the tools and strategies they need to thrive.

Beyond their personal experiences, Avi Quinn has sought wisdom from mental health professionals, educators, and experts in the field of adolescent anxiety to create a comprehensive resource that combines empathy, knowledge, and practical solutions.

As an author, Avi Quinn brings a deep sense of empathy and understanding to the pages of this book. They believe in the power of hope, resilience, and the potential for positive change. It is their hope that this book serves as a beacon of light for those navigating the challenges of anxiety and stress, guiding them towards a path of healing, growth, and well-being.

www.ingramcontent.com/pod-product-compliance
Lightning Source LLC
Chambersburg PA
CBHW070004180726
48002CB00019B/1896